Table of Contents

Introduction

The instant pot is as versatile as it is fun! Enjoy a culinary adventure using recipes based on meat, seafood, vegetarian ingredients! Discover desserts that are easier and more delicious than you thought possible. Whether working and living a busy life, entertaining friends and family, you're sure to find a great many uses for the recipes in this book. Convenience and diversity of ingredients, quick cooking or slow cooking for home cooked meals that basically cook themselves, there is much to find and delight in here!

Chapter 1: Breakfast Recipes

Tomato Poached Eggs (Pressure cooked)

Prep time: 5 minutes

Cooking time: 5 minutes

Ingredients:

- Five eggs
- Five large tomatoes
- Three tablespoons butter, melted to liquid
- ½ teaspoon pepper

Directions:

1. Place one cup of water in the Instant Pot.
2. Hollow out the tomatoes by digging out the inner part of each fruit.
3. Break an egg into each and place each tomato containing egg in an oven safe dish and place said dish into your instant pot.
4. Select pressure cooking and cook on low pressure for 5 minutes.
5. Remove the eggs and top with the butter and pepper. Serve with turkey, ham or beef slices, cheese or as is with toast.

Pressure cooked Boiled

Prep time: 5 minutes

Cooking time: 5 minutes

Ingredients:

- Five eggs

Directions:

1. Place one cup of water in the Instant Pot.
2. Put the eggs in a trivet or steaming container.
3. Set the instant pot to pressure cook and cook on high pressure for five minutes (or less if you prefer runny eggs).
4. Crack and eat on toast, rolls or simply as is with a bit of salt and pepper.

Rich Thyme Eggs

Prep time: 5 minutes

Cooking time: 18 minutes

Ingredients:
- 1 cup heavy cream
- 5 eggs, beaten
- One potato, sliced thinly
- One teaspoon fresh or dried thyme

Directions:
1. Beat the eggs along with the cream.
2. Add in and stir the rest of the ingredients in an oven safe form.
3. Pour a cup of water into the instant pot.
4. Press "manual" and cook for 18 minutes.
5. Serve with bread for a hearty breakfast.

Egg and Bean Breakfast

Prep time: 5 minutes

Cooking time: 18 minutes

Ingredients:
- ½ cup milk
- 5 eggs, beaten
- ½ cup tomato sauce
- One cup cooked white beans
- 2 cloves garlic, chopped
- One teaspoon chili powder

Directions:
1. Beat the eggs along with the milk.
2. Add in and stir the rest of the ingredients in an oven safe form.
3. Pour a cup of water into the instant pot.
4. Press "manual" and cook for 18 minutes.
5. Serve with bread for a hearty breakfast.

Super Cheesy Easy Eggs

Prep time: 5 minutes

Cooking time: 10 minutes

Ingredients:
- ½ cup heavy cream
- 5 eggs, beaten
- One tablespoon cream cheese
- ½ cup Swiss cheese
- ½ cup cheddar cheese
- ½ cup mozzarella cheese
- 2 cloves garlic, chopped
- ½ teaspoon black pepper

Directions:
1. Beat the eggs along with the cream and cream cheese.
2. Add in and stir the rest of the ingredients in an oven safe form.
3. Pour a cup of water into the instant pot.
4. Press "manual" and cook for 18 minutes.
5. Serve with bread for a hearty breakfast.

Mexican Breakfast Casserole

Prep time: 5 minutes or less

Cooking time: 10 minutes

Ingredients:
- ½ cup sour cream
- 5 eggs, beaten
- ½ cup tomato salsa
- One green pepper, chopped into small bits
- One onion, chopped
- One cup pepper jack cheese

Directions:
1. Beat the eggs along with the sour cream.
2. Add in and stir the rest of the ingredients in an oven safe form.
3. Pour a cup of water into the instant pot.
4. Press "manual" and cook for 18 minutes.
5. Serve with tortilla wraps.

Millet Cream Porridge

Prep time: 5 minutes or less

Cooking time: 12 minutes

Ingredients:
- 2 cups millet flakes
- 1 cup water
- 2 cups heavy cream
- 3 tablespoons maple syrup
- One tablespoon coconut oil
- One teaspoon vanilla extract
- One cup almond butter
- One teaspoon cinnamon

Directions:
1. Place all of the ingredients in the instant pot.
2. Select the pressure cooker setting. (Move lever to sealing; consult user's manual if uncertain) Choose high pressure.
3. Set the timer for 2 minutes.
4. When finished cooking, allow to stand for 10 minutes before releasing the cooker (simply turn off the Instant Pot).
5. Serve topped with walnuts, additional maple syrup or your choice of topping.

Breakfast Bread

Prep time: 5 minutes

Cooking time: 25 minutes

Ingredients:

- One teaspoon coconut oil
- 2 cups of flour
- 1 teaspoon baking soda
- 1.5 cups full fat plain yogurt

Directions:

1. Place one cup of water in the Instant Pot.
2. Combine the flour with the baking soda.
3. Stir in the yogurt.
4. Use your hands to knead the dough.
5. Grease an oven safe form (which fits in your instant pot) with the coconut oil.

6. Place the bread dough in the pan and cover with a bit of water. Then cover with aluminum foil (around the whole pan) and place the pan in the instant pot. Cook for 25 minutes on the high pressure setting.
7. Allow the instant pot to release before removing the bread.
8. Serve with butter or with one of the egg recipes in this book.

Blackberry Jam

Prep time: 5 minutes

Cooking time: 6 hours or overnight

Ingredients:

- One pound fresh blackberries
- ¾ cup sugar
- 1 teaspoon lemon juice

Directions:

1. Place all the ingredients in the instant pot and stir.
2. Set the instant pot to slow cook and allow to cook on low for 6 hours or overnight while you sleep.
3. Serve in the morning on homemade bread.

Ginger Lemon Marmalade

Prep time: 5 minutes

Cooking time: 6 hours or overnight

Ingredients:

- 8 large lemons, cut into slices with the skin still on (for this reason it's best to choose organic)
- One cup peeled ginger
- One cup sugar

Directions:

1. Place all the ingredients in the instant pot and stir.
2. Set the instant pot to slow cook and allow to cook on low for 6 hours or overnight while you sleep.

3. Serve in the morning on homemade bread or top on oatmeal or yogurt.

Strawberry Oatmeal

Prep time: 5 minutes

Cooking time: 6 hours or while you sleep

Ingredients:

- 2 cups oats
- 3 cups grassfed milk
- One tablespoon coconut oil
- One tablespoon vanilla extract
- 4 tablespoons honey
- One cup frozen or fresh chopped strawberries
- One pinch himalayan or sea salt

Directions:

1. Place all the ingredients in the instant pot and stir.
2. Set the instant pot to slow cook and allow to cook on low for 6 hours or overnight while you sleep.
3. Serve in the morning on homemade bread.

Cinnamon Pancakes

Prep time: 5 minutes

Cooking time: 5 minutes

Ingredients:

- One cup of flour
- One tablespoon cinnamon
- ¼ teaspoon baking powder
- One pinch sea salt
- One egg
- ½ cup oat milk or grass fed dairy milk
- One tablespoon warmed to liquid coconut oil
- One tablespoon coconut oil to grease the pan with

Directions:

1. Mix the ingredients together until a smooth batter is formed.

2. Grease an oven safe form with the additional coconut oil.
3. First spoon one pancake worth into the form.
4. Top with parchment paper and spoon another pancake onto the parchment paper. Layer until the batter has been used up.
5. Cover with tin foil.
6. Pour one cup of water into the instant pot. Place the form in the instant pot.
7. Cook high pressure for five minutes.
8. Top with syrup or homemade jam.

Müesli Blend

Prep time: 5 minutes

Cooking time: 6 hours or overnight

Ingredients:

- Two cups rolled oats
- One cup cashews
- One cup dried cranberries
- One teaspoon chia seeds
- One tablespoon sunflower seeds
- One cup apple pieces
- Four tablespoons honey or maple syrup
- One tablespoon cinnamon

Directions:

1. Place all of the ingredients in the instant pot. Stir and coat all of the ingredients with the honey or maple syrup.
2. Cook on low on the slow cooker setting for 5-8 hours

Coffee Cake

Prep time: 5 minutes

Cooking time: 5-6 hours

Ingredients:

Topping:

- 1 cup coconut sugar
- ½ cup oat flour
- 4 tablespoons melted butter or coconut oil

Cake:

- 5 tablespoons coconut oil
- 2 cups whole wheat flour (buckwheat for gluten free)
- Two teaspoons baking soda
- Two tablespoons cinnamon
- ¼ teaspoon cloves
- 2 eggs, beaten
- One tablespoon vanilla extract
- One cup apple sauce
- One cup coconut sugar

Directions:

1. Mix the topping in a bowl. Mix the cake ingredients in a separate bowl until smooth.
2. Cover the inside of your instant pot with aluminum foil.
3. Spread the cake batter into your instant pot. Then place the topping on the cake.
4. Set your instant pot to low on the slow cooker setting. Cook for 6 hours (but not more than that as you don't want the cake to dry out.)
5. Serve for breakfast with coffee.

Protein Muffins

Prep time: 5 minutes

Cooking time: 5 minutes

Ingredients:

- 6 eggs, beaten
- One cup bacon, shredded into pieces
- One cup baby spinach
- One cup tomatoes, chopped
- One cup cream cheese
- One cup mozzarella cheese

Directions:

1. Stir the cream cheese in with the beaten eggs.
2. Add the bacon, spinach tomatoes and mozzarella cheese and stir gently.
3. Place the mixture in muffin cups.
4. Put one cup of water in the instant pot.
5. Wrap the muffins in tin foil.

6. Cook on the high pressure setting for 5 minutes.
7. Enjoy as part of a big breakfast or on the go.

Oatmeal

Prep time: 5 minutes

Cooking time: 12 minutes

Ingredients:
- 1 cup steel cut oats
- 2 cups coconut or almond milk
- 3 tablespoons maple syrup
- One teaspoon cinnamon

Directions:
1. Place all of the ingredients in the instant pot.
2. Select the pressure cooker setting. (Move lever to sealing; consult user's manual if uncertain) Choose high pressure.
3. Set the timer for 2 minutes.
4. When finished cooking, allow to stand for 10 minutes before releasing the cooker (simply turn off the Instant Pot).
5. Serve topped with walnuts, additional maple syrup or your choice of topping.

Quinoa Porridge

Prep time: 5 minutes

Cooking time: 12 minutes

Ingredients:
- 1 cup quinoa
- 1 cup water
- 1 cup almond milk
- 3 tablespoons coconut nectar
- One tablespoon coconut oil
- One teaspoon vanilla extract

Directions:
1. Place all of the ingredients in the instant pot.
2. Select the pressure cooker setting. (Move lever to sealing; consult user's manual if uncertain) Choose high pressure.
3. Set the timer for 2 minutes.

4. When finished cooking, allow to stand for 10 minutes before releasing the cooker (simply turn off the Instant Pot).
5. Serve topped with walnuts, additional maple syrup or your choice of topping.

Buckwheat Pear Porridge

Prep time: 5 minutes

Cooking time: 12 minutes

Ingredients:
- 1 cup buckwheat flour or flakes
- 1 cup water
- 1 cup hemp milk
- 3 tablespoons coconut nectar
- One tablespoon coconut oil
- One teaspoon vanilla extract
- One teaspoon cinnamon
- One teaspoon almond butter
- One chopped pear

Directions:
1. Place all of the ingredients in the instant pot.
2. Select the pressure cooker setting. (Move lever to sealing; consult user's manual if uncertain) Choose high pressure.
3. Set the timer for 2 minutes.
4. When finished cooking, allow to stand for 10 minutes before releasing the cooker (simply turn off the Instant Pot).
5. Serve topped with walnuts, additional maple syrup or your choice of topping.

Cherry Rice Porridge

Prep time: 5 minutes

Cooking time: 25 minutes

Ingredients:

- 1 cup rice flour
- 1 cup water
- 1 cup almond milk
- 3 tablespoons maple syrup
- One tablespoon coconut oil
- One teaspoon vanilla extract
- One cup chopped cherries
- One cup almond butter

Directions:

1. Place all of the ingredients in the instant pot.
2. Select the pressure cooker setting. (Move lever to sealing; consult user's manual if uncertain) Choose high pressure.
3. Set the timer for 2 minutes.
4. When finished cooking, allow to stand for 10 minutes before releasing the cooker (simply turn off the Instant Pot).
5. Serve topped with walnuts, additional maple syrup or your choice of topping.

Breakfast Casserole

Prep time: 5 minutes

Cooking time: 8 hours (while you sleep)

Ingredients:

- 5 eggs, beaten
- ½ cup milk
- ¼ teaspoon pepper
- 2 cups pepper jack cheese
- ½ cup chopped red bell peppers
- ¼ cup chopped onions
- ½ cup grated potato
- One cup breakfast sausages, chopped small
- ¼ teaspoon sea salt

Directions:

1. Place all of the ingredients in the instant pot the night before you intend to serve your breakfast casserole.
2. First add the eggs, then stir in the milk. Then add the rest of the ingredients. Stir to combine evenly.
3. Select the slow cooker setting. Set the timer for 8 hours.
4. If you oversleep, no problem. The Instant Pot will keep your meal warm for you. Serve with good bread for a hearty breakfast.

Chapter 2: Poultry Recipes

Spicy Bacon Chicken

Prep time: 5 minutes

Cooking time: 25 minutes

Ingredients:

- Two chicken breasts
- One cup chicken broth
- Two tablespoons chili powder
- Two jalapeno peppers, chopped
- 4 slices bacon, fried crispy
- One cup sour cream

Directions:

1. Pour the chicken broth into the instant pot. Add the jalapeno peppers and chili powder and stir.
2. Place the chicken breasts in the instant pot.
3. Cook on the slow cooker setting for 6-8 hours.
4. Finally, stir in the sour cream and top with the fried chicken for a chicken and sauce meal.

Beans and Chicken Slow Cooked

Prep time: 5 minutes

Cooking time: 6-8 hours

Ingredients:

- ½ cup black beans, soaked overnight and rinsed
- One cup butternut squash, cubed
- Two chicken breasts, cut into pieces
- Three cups chicken broth
- Two cups chopped tomatoes
- One cup green bell pepper, chopped
- One yellow onion, diced
- 3 cloves garlic, diced

- One tablespoon chili powder
- One teaspoon black pepper

Directions:

1. Place all of the ingredients in the instant pot.
2. Cook on the slow cook setting for 6-8 hours.

Chicken and Corn Pot

Prep time: 5 minutes

Cooking time: 6-8 hours

Ingredients:

- Two cups corn
- One cup shredded kale
- Two chicken breasts, cut into pieces
- Three cups chicken broth
- One cup chopped red peppers
- One yellow onion, diced
- 3 cloves garlic, diced
- One tablespoon garlic powder
- One teaspoon black pepper

Directions:

1. Place all of the ingredients in the instant pot.
2. Cook on the slow cook setting for 6-8 hours.
3. Serve with good bread and salad

Mushroom Chicken Stew

Prep time: 5 minutes

Cooking time: 6-8 hours

Ingredients:

- One cup sliced aroma mushrooms (brown crimini mushrooms)
- One cup sour cream
- Two cups chicken broth

- Two chicken breasts, cut into pieces
- One garlic clove, chopped
- Two large potatoes, diced
- One yellow onion, chopped

Directions:

1. Place all of the ingredients in the instant pot.
2. Cook on the slow cook setting for 6-8 hours.
3. Serve with good bread and salad

Chicken Red Wine Pot

Prep time: 5 minutes

Cooking time: 6-8 hours

Ingredients:

- Two chicken breasts
- Two cups chicken broth
- Two tablespoons cornstarch
- ½ cup red wine
- ½ cup chopped rutabaga
- Two garlic cloves, chopped
- One yellow onion, chopped

Directions:

1. Place all of the ingredients in the instant pot.
2. Cook on the slow cook setting for 6-8 hours.
3. Serve with good bread and salad

Thai Coconut Chicken Stew

Prep time: 5 minutes

Cooking time: 6-8 hours

Ingredients:

- Two chicken breasts, cut into pieces
- Two cups chicken broth

- ½ cup coconut milk
- One tablespoon lemongrass powder
- One teaspoon garlic powder
- One cup green beans
- ½ cup red pepper, chopped
- ¼ cup cashew nuts
- One tablespoon chili powder

Directions:

1. Place all of the ingredients in the instant pot.
2. Cook on the slow cook setting for 6-8 hours.
3. Serve with rice.

Chicken and Rice

Prep time: 5 minutes

Cooking time: 6-8 hours

Ingredients:

- Two chicken breasts, cut into pieces
- Three cups chicken broth
- ½ cup rice
- ½ cup carrots
- ½ cup chopped celery root
- 1 onion, chopped
- Two cloves garlic, chopped

Directions:

1. Place all of the ingredients in the instant pot.
2. Cook on the slow cook setting for 6-8 hours.

Indian Curry Chicken

Prep time: 5 minutes

Cooking time: 6-8 hours

Ingredients:

- Two chicken breasts, cut into pieces
- Two cups chicken broth
- ½ cup coconut milk
- Two tablespoons cornstarch
- One tablespoon curcumin powder
- One tablespoon fenugreek powder
- One tablespoon garlic powder
- One teaspoon chilli powder
- Two potatoes, cubed
- Two tomatoes, chopped
- One carrot, chopped
- One cup spinach

Directions:

1. Place all of the ingredients in the instant pot.
2. Cook on the slow cook setting for 6-8 hours.
3. Serve with rice.

Chinese Duck Stew Sweet and Sour

Prep time: 5 minutes

Cooking time: 6-8 hours

Ingredients:

- One cup duck breasts, cut into pieces
- Two cups chicken broth
- Two tablespoons lemon juice
- One tablespoon orange juice
- One tablespoon honey
- Two tablespoons chili powder
- Two tablespoons cornstarch
- ½ cup shredded carrots
- One tablespoon black pepper
- One cup green beans

Directions:

1. Place all of the ingredients in the instant pot.
2. Cook on the slow cook setting for 6-8 hours.
3. Serve with rice.

Pumpkin Risotto

Prep time: 5 minutes

Cooking time: 15 minutes

Ingredients:
- Four cups chicken broth from previous recipe (or another)
- 3 tablespoons olive oil
- One teaspoon sage (fresh or dried)
- 3 cups diced (with seeds removed) hokkaido pumpkin
- One cup cream cheese
- 2 cups risotto rice
- 2 cloves garlic, chopped
- One yellow onion, chopped
- Two tablespoons white wine

Directions:

1. Use the sautee setting to sautee the onion and garlic in the olive oil. Add the pumpkin and sautee for one minute.
2. Stir in the spices and add the white wine. Stir.
3. Add the chicken broth and the risotto. Stir.
4. Cook on high pressure for 7 minutes.
5. Lower pressure and cook for an additional three minutes.
6. Allow to release pressure naturally and stir in the cream cheese.

Warm Chicken Salad

Prep time: 5 minutes

Cooking time: 30 minutes

Ingredients:
- One whole chicken or one pound chicken breasts
- One cup water
- One cup mayonnaise or sour cream
- One teaspoon garlic powder

- One teaspoon black pepper
- 3 cups baby spinach
- 3 tomatoes, diced
- One avocado, sliced

Directions:

1. Place the chicken and water in the Instant Pot.
2. Use the high pressure setting to cook. Press in the manual button to add minutes for a total of 30 minute cooking time or press the poultry button.
3. In the meantime, prepare the salad by combining the spinach, tomatoes and avocado in a salad bowl.
4. Mix the mayo or sour cream with the garlic powder and black pepper.
5. When the chicken is ready, open the Instant Pot. Cut the chicken into pieces (removing the bone if not boneless) and mix in the mayo or sour cream dressing.
6. Serve warm over the salad.

Chicken Mozzarella Parmesan

Prep time: 5 minutes

Cooking time: 6-8 hours

Ingredients:

- Two chicken breasts, cut into pieces
- One cup chicken broth
- One cup tomato sauce
- Two cloves garlic, chopped
- One tablespoon black pepper
- One cup mozzarella cheese
- Two tablespoons parmesan cheese

Directions:

1. Place all of the ingredients except the mozzarella cheese in the instant pot.
2. Cook on the slow cook setting for 6-8 hours.
3. Top with the mozzarella cheese.
4. Serve with good bread and salad

Spicy Chicken and Chickpeas

Prep time: 5 minutes

Cooking time: 6-8 hours

Ingredients:

- Two chicken breasts, cut into pieces
- One cup chicken broth
- One cup tomato sauce or tomato soup
- One cup rinsed and soaked (overnight or for 8 hours) chickpeas
- One teaspoon garlic powder
- One tablespoon chili powder

Directions:

1. Place all of the ingredients in the instant pot.
2. Cook on the slow cook setting for 6-8 hours.
3. Serve with good bread and salad

Chicken and Noodle Casserole

Prep time: 5 minutes

Cooking time: 6-8 hours

Ingredients:

- Two chicken breasts, cut into pieces
- Two cups chicken broth
- One cup soy noodles (don't become soggy like regular noodles do, when slow cooked)
- One cup sour cream
- One yellow onion, chopped
- One cup asparagus, chopped into bite-sized pieces

Directions:

1. Place all of the ingredients in the instant pot.
2. Cook on the slow cook setting for 6-8 hours.
3. Serve with good bread and salad

Beer Sauce Chicken (high pressure)

Prep time: 5 minutes

Cooking time: 8 minutes

Ingredients:

- Two chicken breasts, cut into pieces
- One cup beef broth
- ½ cup dark beer
- One tablespoon garlic powder
- One tablespoon black pepper

Directions:

1. Place all of the ingredients in the instant pot.
2. Cook on high pressure setting for 8 minutes.
3. Allow pressure to naturally release.
4. Serve with salad and bread.

Guinness Chicken, slow cooked

Prep time: 5 minutes

Cooking time: 6-8 hours

Ingredients:

- Two chicken breasts, cut into pieces
- Two cups chicken broth
- ½ cup guinness stout
- Two onions, chopped
- Two cloves garlic, chopped
- Two potatoes, cubed

Directions:

1. Place all of the ingredients in the instant pot.
2. Cook on the slow cook setting for 6-8 hours.
3. Serve with good bread and salad

Green Pepper Chicken

Prep time: 5 minutes

Cooking time: 8 minutes

Ingredients:

- Two chicken breasts, cut into pieces
- Two cups chicken broth
- ½ cup sour cream
- One green pepper, sliced lengthwise
- One red pepper, sliced lengthwise
- One red onion, sliced into rings
- Two tablespoons garlic powder

Directions:

1. Place all of the ingredients in the instant pot.
2. Cook on high pressure setting for 8 minutes.
3. Allow pressure to naturally release.
4. Serve with salad and bread.

Chicken Frikadelle (chicken patties)

Prep time: 10 minutes

Cooking time: 10 minutes

Ingredients:

- One pound ground chicken meat
- One cup almond flour
- Three eggs, beaten
- Two tablespoons garlic powder
- One tablespoon black pepper

Directions:

1. Combine the ingredients together in a bowl.
2. Put one cup of water in the instant pot
3. Put the patties in an oven safe dish (separated by parchment paper). Cover the dish with tin foil.
4. Pressure cook on high heat for 10 minutes.
5. Serve as burgers on bread or with salad for a low carb meal.

Turkey Tomato Casserole

Prep time: 5 minutes

Cooking time: 6-8 hours

Ingredients:

- One turkey breast
- Two cups turkey broth
- ½ cup tomato sauce
- One onion, chopped
- One cup tomatoes, chopped
- Two cups diced potatoes

Directions:

1. Place all of the ingredients in the instant pot.
2. Cook on the slow cook setting for 6-8 hours.
3. Serve with salad and bread.

Vegetables and Pulled Turkey

Prep time: 5 minutes

Cooking time: 5 minutes

Ingredients:

- Two cups pulled turkey (high pressure pre cook whole turkey, strip off meat and use in this recipe)
- Two cups turkey broth (or vegetable broth)
- One cup tomato sauce
- One cup peas
- One cup chopped carrots
- One chopped onion
- One cubed potato

Directions:

1. Place all of the ingredients in the instant pot.
2. Cook on high pressure setting for five minutes.
3. Allow pressure to naturally release.
4. Serve with salad and bread.

Whole Chicken

Prep time: 5 minutes

Cooking time: 20 minutes

Ingredients:

- One cup water
- One whole chicken

Directions:

1. Pour the water into the instant pot.
2. Place the chicken in the water.
3. Select the high pressure setting on the instant pot.
4. Cook on high pressure for twenty minutes. Allow the pressure valve to release on its own.
5. Optionally cook in chicken broth and add herbs like sage, thyme and rosemary for an extra flavorful chicken.

Turkey Burgers

Prep time: 10 minutes

Cooking time: 10 minutes

Ingredients:

- One pound ground turkey meat
- One cup sour cream
- Two eggs
- One cup wholegrain flour
- One tablespoon dill
- One tablespoon onion powder.

Directions:

1. Combine the ingredients together in a bowl.
2. Put one cup of water in the instant pot
3. Put the patties in an oven safe dish (separated by parchment paper). Cover the dish with tin foil.
4. Pressure cook on high heat for 10 minutes.
5. Serve as burgers on bread or with salad for a low carb meal.

Chapter 3: Meat Recipes

Roast

Prep time: 10 minutes

Cooking time: 6-8 hours

Ingredients:

- Two cups beef broth
- One cup sour cream
- One beef roast

Directions:

1. Place all of the ingredients in the instant pot.
2. Cook on the slow cook setting for 6-8 hours (check progress or simply allow to cook during your work day).
3. Serve with salad and bread.

Slow Cooked Potato Broccoli Bacon Casserole

Prep time: 10 minutes

Cooking time: 6-8 hours (can be held warm during your work day)

Ingredients:

- Four cups chicken broth
- Three cups potatoes, diced (but not too small)
- Two cups broccoli florets
- One cup crispy bacon, shredded into bits
- One cup sour cream
- Three cloves garlic, chopped
- One tablespoon butter
- Two teaspoons black pepper

Directions:

1. Use the sautee setting to sautee the garlic in the butter.
2. Set to slow cook setting for 6 hours and add the rest of the ingredients.
3. When ready to eat, top with shredded cheese.

Bacon Rice

Prep time: 10 minutes

Cooking time: 15 minutes

Ingredients:

- Four cups beef broth broth
- 3 tablespoons olive oil
- One teaspoon thyme
- 3 cups crispy bacon shredded into bits
- One cup sour cream
- brown rice
- 2 cloves garlic, chopped
- One yellow onion, chopped
- One cup chopped green beans

Directions:

1. Use the saute setting to saute the onion and garlic in the olive oil.
2. Add the rest of the ingredients and set to high pressure and cook for 10.
3. Allow pressure to release. Stir and enjoy.

Meatloaf with Herbs

Prep time: 10 minutes

Cooking time: 40 minutes

Ingredients:

- 2 pounds or two packages of ground beef
- 2 eggs
- One cup almond flour
- One teaspoon thyme
- One teaspoon rosemary
- One teaspoon garlic powder
- Three tablespoons olive oil

Directions:

1. Combine the beef, eggs, flour and seasonings in a large mixing bowl. Use a wooden spoon or your hands to combine everything well and evenly.
2. Coat the Instant pot with olive oil.
3. Put the meatloaf mixture into the instant pot. Pack in firmly with your hands or the spoon to form the meatloaf.

4. Set for 40 minutes on the meat/setting on normal pressure.
5. Open instant pot when settings show it is safe to do so.
6. Serve with mashed potatoes and salad.

Slow Cooked Goulash

Prep time: 10 minutes

Cooking time: 6-8 hours (can be held warm during your work day)

Ingredients:

- Four cups beef broth
- One cup cubed beef steak
- Two cups tomato sauce
- 3 tablespoons spicy paprika powder
- One cup chopped potatoes
- One cup chopped red bell pepper
- Four cloves chopped garlic
- One tablespoon butter

Directions:

1. Use the sautee setting to sautee the garlic in the butter.
2. Set to slow cook setting for 6 hours and add the rest of the ingredients.
3. When ready to eat, serve with bread and/or top with sour cream.

Slow Cooked Shepherd's Pie

Prep time: 15 minutes

Cooking time: 4 hours (can be held warm during your work day)

Ingredients:

- One pound of ground beef, or other ground meat
- 5 potatoes, cooked and mashed
- One cup diced carrots
- ½ cup thawed frozen peas
- ½ cup thawed frozen green beans
- One teaspoon onion powder
- One teaspoon garlic powder
- One tablespoon Worcestershire sauce
- One onion, diced
- Two tablespoons butter
- One tablespoon tomato paste

Directions:

1. Place the meat in the Instant Pot along with the butter and onions and Worcestershire sauce. Set to high pressure on the pressure cooker setting and cook for 8 minutes.
2. While that is cooking, combine the carrots, peas and green beans along with the tomato paste, onion and garlic powder in a mixing bowl.
3. When the meat is finished cooking, simply place the vegetables on top. Top with the mashed potatoes and set to slow cook for 4 hours. Serve when you're ready to eat.

Roast Beef Beer Roast

Prep time: 10 minutes

Cooking time: 6-8 hours

Ingredients:

- Two cups beef broth
- One cup sour cream
- One beef roast (a pound or more of meat)
- One cup dark beer
- Two cups cubed potatoes
- One yellow onion, chopped

Directions:

1. Place all of the ingredients in the instant pot.
2. Cook on the slow cook setting for 6-8 hours.
3. Serve with salad and bread.

Cranberry Roast Beef

Prep time: 10 minutes

Cooking time: 6-8 hours

Ingredients:

- Two cups beef broth
- ½ cup cranberries
- ½ cup chopped parsnips
- ½ cup chopped red onion
- One teaspoon black pepper
- One beef roast

Directions:

1. Place all of the ingredients in the instant pot.
2. Cook on the slow cook setting for 6-8 hours.
3. Serve with salad and bread.

Beef Tomato Roast

Prep time: 10 minutes

Cooking time: 6-8 hours

Ingredients:

- Two cups beef broth
- One cup tomato soup
- One beef roast, one pound or more
- One teaspoon black pepper
- One red bell pepper, sliced
- One cup sun dried tomatoes

Directions:

1. Place all of the ingredients in the instant pot.
2. Cook on the slow cook setting for 6-8 hours.
3. Serve with salad and bread.

Potato and Beef Roast Classic

Prep time: 10 minutes

Cooking time: 6-8 hours

Ingredients:

- Two cups beef broth
- One cup sour cream
- One beef roast
- One cup potatoes, chopped
- One cup carrots, chopped
- One teaspoon black pepper

Directions:

1. Place all of the ingredients in the instant pot.
2. Cook on the slow cook setting for 6-8 hours. Check progress after six hours. Allow to cook on low for all 8 if necessary according to your schedule.
3. Serve with salad and bread.

Vegetable Beef Roast

Prep time: 10 minutes

Cooking time: 6-8 hours

Ingredients:

- Two cups beef broth
- One cup sour cream
- One beef roast
- ¼ cup carrots
- ¼ cup potatoes
- ¼ cup parsnips
- ¼ cup green beans
- ¼ cup kale

Directions:

1. Place all of the ingredients in the instant pot.
2. Cook on the slow cook setting for 6-8 hours.
3. Serve with salad and bread.

Venison Stew

Prep time: 10 minutes

Cooking time: 6-8 hours

Ingredients:

- Two cups beef broth
- One cup sour cream
- One pound venison (deer meat)
- One teaspoon black pepper
- One cup chopped potatoes
- One cup green peas

Directions:

1. Place all of the ingredients in the instant pot.
2. Cook on the slow cook setting for 6-8 hours.
3. Serve with salad and bread.

Beef Stew

Prep time: 10 minutes

Cooking time: 6-8 hours

Ingredients:

- Four cups beef broth
- Two cups cubed beef
- ½ cup cubed potatoes
- ½ cup cubed carrots
- One tablespoon black pepper
- ¼ cup chopped yellow onion

Directions:

1. Place all of the ingredients in the instant pot.
2. Cook on the slow cook setting for 6-8 hours.
3. Serve with salad and bread.

Indian Spices Beef Stew

Prep time: 10 minutes

Cooking time: 6-8 hours

Ingredients:

- Four cups beef broth
- One cup sour cream
- Two cups cubed beef
- ½ cup cubed potatoes
- ½ cup cubed carrots
- One tablespoon black pepper
- ¼ cup chopped yellow onion
- ½ cup peas
- ½ cup chickpeas

- One tablespoon curcumin powder
- One tablespoon garlic powder
- One tablespoon chili powder
- One tablespoon fenugreek powder
- One tablespoon black pepper

Directions:

1. Place all of the ingredients in the instant pot.
2. Cook on the slow cook setting for 6-8 hours.
3. Serve with salad and bread.

Cauliflower Cream Beef Stew

Prep time: 10 minutes

Cooking time: 6-8 hours

Ingredients:

- Three cups beef broth
- Two cups cubed beef
- Two cups coconut milk (or full fat cream)
- Two heads of cauliflower, chopped
- One tablespoon black pepper
- ¼ cup chopped yellow onion

Directions:

1. Place all of the ingredients in the instant pot.
2. Cook on the slow cook setting for 6-8 hours.
3. Serve with salad and bread.

Broccoli Potato Cream Beef Stew

Prep time: 10 minutes

Cooking time: 6-8 hours

Ingredients:

- Three cups beef broth
- Two cups cubed beef

- Two cups coconut milk (or full fat cream)
- One head of broccoli, separated from the large stem
- Two cups cubed potatoes
- Four cloves of garlic, chopped

Directions:

1. Place all of the ingredients in the instant pot.
2. Cook on the slow cook setting for 6-8 hours.
3. Serve with salad and bread.

Beef Pasta (high pressure)

Prep time: 10 minutes

Cooking time: 15 minutes

Ingredients:

- One package whole grain spiral noodles
- One package (½ pound) of ground beef
- One cup shredded cheddar cheese
- Two cups tomato sauce
- One cup spinach
- One chopped onion
- ½ stick butter

Directions:

1. Set to sautee on the instant pot and saute the onion in the butter.
2. Place the beef in the instant pot and set to high pressure.
3. Open pressure cooker and stir.
4. Add the noodles and pour in some water, but only enough to cover the noodles.
5. Set the heat to high but pressure valve to low. Cook the noodles for five minutes.
6. Stir and drain any excess water remaining.
7. Set instant pot to warm and stir in the tomato sauce and spinach. Top with the cheese.

Beef Taco Casserole

Prep time: 10 minutes

Cooking time: 15 minutes

Ingredients:

- One pound ground beef
- One package corn noodles (gluten free noodles are usually made of corn)
- Two cups shredded cheddar cheese
- Two cups tomato sauce
- One package of taco spices
- One tablespoon crushed red pepper
- One chopped onion
- ½ stick butter
-

Directions:

1. Set to saute and saute the onion in the butter.
2. Place the beef in the instant pot and set to high pressure.
3. Open pressure cooker and stir.
4. Add the noodles and pour in some water, but only enough to cover the noodles.
5. Set the heat to high but pressure valve to low. Cook the noodles for five minutes.
6. Stir and drain any excess water remaining.
7. Set instant pot to warm and stir in the tomato sauce and spices. Top with the cheese.

Beef Stroganoff

Prep time: 10 minutes

Cooking time: 15 minutes

Ingredients:

- Two cups beef strips (steak tips)
- 3 tablespoons olive oil
- One tablespoon flour
- One chopped onion
- 2 minced garlic cloves
- One cup sliced mushrooms
- Two tablespoons tomato paste
- Two cups sour cream
- 3 tablespoons Worcestershire sauce

- Two cups beef broth
- One package egg noodles, cooked
- ¼ teaspoon salt
- ¼ teaspoon pepper

Directions:

1. Place the flour, salt, pepper and beef strips in a bowl. Coat the beef with the flour and seasoning.
2. Put the instant pot on low heat and low pressure to cook the meat for 10 minutes.
3. Add in all of the rest of the ingredients except the sour cream.
4. Seal and cook for 18 minutes at medium pressure.
5. Stir in the sour cream last.
6. Serve along with the noodles. (You may place the noodles in the instant pot with the stroganoff sauce and meat to warm everything up).

Taco Salad

Prep time: 5 minutes

Cooking time: 15 minutes

Ingredients:

- One pound ground beef
- ¼ cup water
- One tablespoon chili powder
- 2 tablespoons taco sauce
- One tablespoon garlic powder
- One head of iceberg lettuce, shredded into bite sized pieces
- Two cups cheese
- Two tomatoes, diced
- Two tablespoons sour cream

Directions:

1. Place the ground beef, water, chili powder, garlic and taco sauce in the Instant Pot.
2. Use the high pressure setting to cook. Press in the manual button to add minutes for a total of 15 minute cooking time.
3. In the meantime, prepare the salad by combining the lettuce, cheese, tomatoes and sour cream. Optionally, add avocado or guacamole.
4. When the 15 minutes is up, release the valve or wait until Instant Pot unlocks and turn off and open.
5. Place the meat on top of the other ingredients and serve hot with taco sauce or salsa with optional tortilla chips.

Beef and Spicy Beans

Prep time: 10 minutes

Cooking time: 6-8 hours

Ingredients:

- One cup black beans, soaked overnight and drained
- Two cups beef strips
- Two cups beef broth
- One cup tomato sauce
- ½ potatoes, cubed
- ¼ chopped carrots
- Two tablespoons crushed red pepper
- One teaspoon black pepper
- One tablespoon chili powder
- One tablespoon garlic powder.

Directions:

1. Place all of the ingredients in the instant pot.
2. Cook on the slow cook setting for 6-8 hours.
3. Serve with salad and bread.

Beef Risotto

Prep time: 10 minutes

Cooking time: 15 minutes

Ingredients:

- 2 tablespoons olive oil
- One tablespoon butter
- 2 cups risotto rice
- 4 1/2 cups beef broth
- One cup cream cheese
- 2 tablespoons parmesan
- Two cups beef steak tips
- One yellow onion, finely chopped
- 2 cloves garlic, finely chopped

Directions:

1. Set the instant pot to sautee. Add the oil, butter, onions and garlic and stir.
2. Next, add the beef, rice and broth. Cover and lock.
3. Cook on high pressure for 8 minutes. Allow pressure to release.
4. Test the rice to be sure it has reached the desired consistency. If not, then cook for an additional two minutes.
5. Stir in the cream cheese and parmesan. Garnish with parsley and serve optionally with a glass of red wine.

Creamy Beef Noodles

Prep time: 10 minutes

Cooking time: 15 minutes

Ingredients:

- One package penne pasta
- Two cups beef broth
- One cup steak tips
- One cup cream cheese
- Two tablespoons full fat cream
- ½ cup chopped red peppers
- ½ cup sliced mushrooms
- One tablespoon garlic powder
- One tablespoon onion powder
- One onion, chopped
- Two tablespoons butter

Directions:

1. Set to saute on the instant pot and saute the onion in the butter.
2. Place the beef in the instant pot and set to high pressure.
3. Open pressure cooker and stir.
4. Add the noodles, pepper and mushroom and spices and pour in the beef broth.
5. Set the heat to high but pressure valve to low. Cook the noodles for five minutes.
6. Stir in the cream cheese and full fat cream. Allow to stand for five minutes.

Beef and Potato Casserole

Prep time: 10 minutes

Cooking time: 15 minutes

Ingredients:

- One pound ground beef
- Two cups potatoes, cubed
- Two cups shredded pepper jack cheese
- Two cups tomato sauce
- Two cups beef broth
- Two tablespoons butter
- One yellow onion, chopped

Directions:

1. Set to sautee and sautee the onion in the butter.
2. Place the beef in the instant pot and set to high pressure.
3. Open pressure cooker and stir.
4. Add the potatoes and then the beef broth.
5. Set the heat to high but pressure valve to low. Cook the meat and potatoes for five minutes.
6. Stir.
7. Set instant pot to warm and stir in the tomato sauce and spices. Top with the cheese.

Beef and Zucchini noodles (low carb)

Prep time: 5 minutes

Cooking time: 15 minutes

Ingredients:

- One pound ground beef
- Two cups shredded pepper jack cheese
- One cup sour cream
- Three tablespoons butter
- Three cloves garlic, chopped
- Three large zucchini, cut into noodles with a mandolin or spiralizer

Directions:

1. Set to saute and saute the garlic in the butter.

2. Place the beef in the instant pot and set to high pressure and medium heat. Cook for 8 minutes or until the meat is browned.
3. Open pressure cooker and stir.
4. Add the sour cream, cheese and zucchini noodles.
5. Cook on high pressure, medium heat for 4 minutes.
6. Stir and serve.

Venison Chili

Prep time: 10 minutes

Cooking time: 6-8 hours

Ingredients:

- One cup black beans, soaked overnight and drained
- One pound ground venison (deer meat)
- Two cups beef broth
- One cup tomato sauce
- One red bell pepper, chopped
- ¼ chopped carrots
- Two tablespoons crushed red pepper
- One teaspoon black pepper
- One tablespoon chili powder
- One tablespoon garlic powder.

Directions:

1. Place all of the ingredients in the instant pot.
2. Cook on the slow cook setting for 6-8 hours.
3. Serve with salad and bread.

Chapter 4: Fish and Seafood

Seafood Stew

Prep time: 10 minutes

Cooking time: 6-8 hours

Ingredients:

- One cup chopped yellow onions
- ½ cup chopped celery
- One cup chopped tomatoes
- 6 cloves garlic, chopped
- One pound swordfish, cut into bite-sized pieces
- One cup shrimp
- 3 cups vegetable broth

Directions:

1. Place all of the ingredients in the instant pot.
2. Cook on the slow cook setting for 6-8 hours.
3. Serve with salad and bread.

Slow Cooked Salmon

Prep time: 5-10 minutes

Cooking time: 6-8 hours or while you are at work Ingredients

Ingredients:

- 1 pound salmon with skin on
- parchment paper
- salt and pepper
- One tablespoon olive oil
- sliced lemon
- one teaspoon thyme
- 3 cups vegetable broth
- one tablespoon soy sauce

Directions:

1. Place the vegetable broth and soy sauce in the Instant Pot.

2. Rub the salmon with salt and pepper, thyme and olive oil. Top with slices of lemon and wrap in the parchment paper. (You will need to slice the salmon into filets to fit one pound of fish into your Instant Pot).
3. Use the slow cooker function to cook for 6 hours. The Instant Pot will keep your food warm after that if you can't serve your fish right away.
4. Serve with potatoes and salad.

Lemon Pepper Cod Fish

Prep time: 10 minutes

Cooking time: 2.5 hours

Ingredients:

- Five cod filets
- ½ cup butter
- ½ cup lemon juice
- One tablespoon black pepper

Directions:

1. Combine the melted butter, lemon juice and black pepper.
2. Place a cod filet in parchment paper. Cover in the butter and lemon juice mixture. Wrap the fish.
3. Repeat the process until all of the fish are wrapped.
4. Slow cook for 2 and a half hours.

Chowder Slow Cooked

Prep time: 10 minutes

Cooking time: 6-8 hours

Ingredients:

- One celeriac (celery root), cubed
- One cup potatoes, diced
- One chopped onion
- One celery stalk, chopped
- 2 tablespoons cornstarch
- 3 salmon filets, cut into one inch pieces
- 2 cups full fat cream
- One cup shrimp
- One teaspoon black pepper

Directions:

1. Place all of the ingredients in the instant pot.
2. Cook on the slow cook setting for 6-8 hours.
3. Serve with salad and bread.

Slow cooked Shrimp stew

Prep time: 10 minutes

Cooking time: 6-8 hours

Ingredients:

- Two pounds shrimp
- 6 cups vegetable broth
- One cup celery root, chopped
- One cup celery stalks, chopped
- One fennel bulb, chopped
- One carrot, chopped
- One red bell pepper, chopped
- One green bell pepper, chopped
- One yellow onion, chopped
- 6 cloves garlic, chopped
- ½ cup cornstarch
- One tablespoon pepper

Directions:

1. Place all of the ingredients in the instant pot and stir, being sure to remove any clumps from the flour using a whisk (add slowly to prevent clumping).
2. Cook on the slow cook setting for 6-8 hours.
3. Serve with salad and bread.

Garlic Butter Sword Fish

Prep time: 10 minutes

Cooking time: 2.5 hours

Ingredients:

- Five sword fish filets
- ½ cup melted butter
- 6 cloves garlic, chopped
- One tablespoon black pepper

Directions:

1. Combine the melted butter, garlic and black pepper in a mixing bowl.
2. Place a cod filet in parchment paper. Cover in the butter and lemon juice mixture. Wrap the fish.
3. Repeat the process until all of the fish are wrapped.
4. Slow cook for 2 and a half hours.

Shrimp and Rice

Prep time: 10 minutes

Cooking time: 6-8 hours

Ingredients:

- Two pounds shrimp with tales removed
- 1 cups instant rice
- 4 cups vegetable broth
- One onion, chopped
- Six cloves garlic, chopped
- One tablespoon black pepper

Directions:

1. Place the ingredients in the instant pot.
2. Stir to distribute the ingredients evenly.
3. Allow to cook for 6-8 hours.

Lemon Coriander Salmon

Prep time: 10 minutes

Cooking time: 3 hours

Ingredients:

- Four salmon filets
- One cup fresh coriander, chopped and de-stemmed
- 3 cloves garlic, chopped
- ½ cup butter
- ½ cup lemon juice
- One tablespoon black pepper

Directions:

1. Coat the instant pot with the butter.
2. Stir the coriander, garlic, lemon juice and pepper in a mixing bowl.
3. Put the salmon filets into the instant pot and pour the mixture onto the fish.
4. Cook on low heat on the slow cook setting for three hours.

Maple Sweet Cod

Prep time: 10 minutes

Cooking time: 3 hours

Ingredients:

- Five cod filets
- 1 cup real maple syrup
- ½ cup tamari (or soy sauce)
- 4 cloves garlic, chopped
- ½ cup butter
- ½ cup lemon juice
- One tablespoon black pepper

Directions:

1. Coat the instant pot with the butter.
2. Stir the tamari, maple syrup, garlic, lemon juice and black pepper in a bowl.
3. Put the salmon filets into the instant pot. Pour the mixture onto the salmon.
4. Cook on low heat on the slow cook setting for three hours.

Tilapia Au Gratin

Prep time: 10 minutes

Cooking time: 3 hours

Ingredients:

- 6 tilapia filets
- One stick of butter
- Three tablespoons flour
- 1 ½ cups full fat cream
- 2 cups shredded cheddar cheese
- One tablespoon black pepper

Directions:

1. Melt the butter in the instant pot. Set to "warm" and add the flour slowly, as well as the cream, cheese, and pepper.
2. Place the fish in the instant pot and cover with the cheese sauce.
3. Cook on the slow cook setting for three hours,

Slow cooked Crab dip

Prep time: 5 minutes

Cooking time: 3 hours

Ingredients:

- Two cups crab meat
- 3 cups cream cheese
- 1 cup sour cream
- One tablespoon garlic powder
- One tablespoon chopped scallions
- One tablespoon black pepper

Directions:

1. Place all of the ingredients in the instant pot.
2. Slow cook for three hours.
3. Serve with bread ,vegetables or chips as an appetizer

Shrimp and Sausage

Prep time: 5 minutes

Cooking time: 6 hours

Ingredients:

- Three celery stalks, chopped
- Five cloves garlic, chopped
- Two tablespoons chili powder
- One tablespoon paprika powder
- One tablespoon onion powder
- 4 cups chicken broth
- Two pounds peeled shrimp
- Three spicy sausages (kielbasa) cut into bite-sized pieces

Directions:

1. Put all the ingredients in the instant pot and stir.
2. Set the instant pot to slow cook and cook for six hours.
3. Serve while hot, along with good bread or with salad. Garnish with parsley.

Barbeque Salmon with Rice

Prep time: 10 minutes

Cooking time: 6-8 hours

Ingredients:

- 4 filets salmon
- 1 cup instant rice
- 4 cups chicken stock
- One onion, chopped
- Six cloves garlic, chopped
- One tablespoon black pepper
- Three tablespoons barbeque sauce
- One carrot, chopped

Directions:

1. Place the ingredients in the instant pot.

2. Stir to distribute the ingredients evenly.
3. Allow to cook for 6-8 hours.

Seafood Paella

Prep time: 10 minutes

Cooking time: 8 minutes

Ingredients:

- Two pounds shrimp with tails removed
- 1 cups instant rice
- 2 cups vegetable broth
- One onion, chopped
- ¼ cup lemon juice
- One teaspoon crushed red pepper
- ¼ cup parsley (fresh)
- Six cloves garlic, chopped
- One tablespoon black pepper
- ½ cup parmesan
- One cup mozzarella cheese

Directions:

1. Place the ingredients in the instant pot.
2. Cook on the high pressure setting for 6 minutes. Allow the pressure to release on its own before opening.
3. Sprinkle with parmesan and mozzarella cheese.

Seafood and Chickpea Pot

Prep time: 10 minutes

Cooking time: 15 minutes

Ingredients:

- One cup chopped scallions
- One chopped carrot
- One pound shrimp
- Two tablespoons black pepper
- Two cups vegetable broth
- Two cod filets

- One cup chickpeas, soaked and drained

Directions:

1. Place the ingredients in the instant pot.
2. Set to high pressure and cook for 12 minutes.
3. Allow pressure to release before opening.
4. Top with tomatoes and cheddar cheese, if so desired.

Clam and Kidney Beans

Prep time: 10 minutes

Cooking time: 15 minutes

Ingredients:

- Two cups kidney beans, soaked overnight and rinsed
- One chopped carrot
- Two tablespoons black pepper
- Three cloves chopped garlic
- One potato, cubed
- ½ cup sun dried tomatoes, chopped
- One cup clam meat

Directions:

1. Place the ingredients in the instant pot.
2. Set to high pressure and cook for 12 minutes.
3. Allow pressure to release before opening.
4. Top with tomatoes and cheddar cheese, if so desired.

Pressure cooked orange salmon

Prep time: 10 minutes

Cooking time: 15 minutes

Ingredients:

- 4 salmon filets
- One cup orange juice
- Two tablespoons cornstarch

- One teaspoon grated orange peel
- One teaspoon black pepper

Directions:

1. Place the ingredients in the instant pot.
2. Set to high pressure and cook for 12 minutes.
3. Allow pressure to release before opening.

Pressure Cooked Lobster

Prep time: 5 minutes

Cooking time: 7 minutes

Ingredients:

- 2 Lobster
- One cup water
- One cup white wine

Directions:

1. Place the ingredients in the instant pot.
2. Set to high pressure and cook for 7 minutes.
3. Allow pressure to release before opening.
4. Serve with melted butter

Pressure Cooked Crab Legs

Prep time: 5 minutes

Cooking time: 7 minutes

Ingredients:

- 2 pounds of crab legs
- One cup water
- One cup white wine
- One cup melted butter
- One lemon, sliced into wedges

Directions:

1. Place the water, wine and crab legs in the instant pot.
2. Set to high pressure and cook for 7 minutes.
3. Allow pressure to release before opening.
4. Serve with melted butter and optionally lemon.

Herbed Chicken Shrimp Risotto Pressure Cooker

Prep time: 10 minutes

Cooking time: 8 minutes

Ingredients:

- Two pounds shrimp with tails removed
- 1 cups instant rice
- 2 cups vegetable broth
- One onion, chopped
- One cup chicken breast, cut into strips
- ¼ cup lemon juice
- One teaspoon crushed red pepper
- ¼ cup parsley (fresh)
- ¼ cup fresh dill
- Six cloves garlic, chopped
- One tablespoon black pepper
- ½ cup parmesan
- One cup mozzarella cheese

Directions:

1. Place the ingredients in the instant pot.
2. Cook on the high pressure setting for 8 minutes. Allow the pressure to release on its own before opening.
3. Sprinkle with parmesan and mozzarella cheese.

Jambalaya

Prep time: 10 minutes

Cooking time: 8 minutes

Ingredients:

- Two pounds shrimp with tails removed
- 1 cups instant rice
- 2 cups vegetable broth
- One onion, chopped
- One cup chicken breast, cut into strips
- One pound cooked spicy sausage, sliced
- 4 cloves chopped garlic
- One green bell pepper, chopped
- 2 tablespoons creole seasoning

Directions:

1. Place the ingredients in the instant pot.
2. Cook on the high pressure setting for 8 minutes. Allow the pressure to release on its own before opening.
3. Sprinkle with your choice of cheese, if so desired.

Chapter 5: Vegetable Recipes

Vegetarian Gumbo

Prep time: 10 minutes

Cooking time: 8 minutes

Ingredients:

- Three tablespoons olive oil
- One red bell pepper, chopped
- One cup kidney beans, soaked overnight and rinsed
- One cup sliced crimini mushrooms
- Three cloves garlic, chopped finely
- Two zucchini, sliced
- Two tablespoons tamari sauce
- Two cups vegetable broth
- 1 teaspoon black pepper

Directions:

1. Place the ingredients in the instant pot.
2. Cook on the high pressure setting for 8 minutes. Allow the pressure to release on its own before opening.
3. Sprinkle with your choice of cheese, if so desired.

Spaghetti Squash and Sauce

Prep time: 10 minutes

Cooking time: 9 minutes

Ingredients:

- 1 spaghetti squash, cut in half width-wise
- One cup water
- 2 cups of your favorite sauce (tomato sauce, alfredo sauce, olive oil and garlic)

Directions:

1. Place all of the ingredients in the instant pot.

2. Select the pressure cooker setting. (Move lever to sealing; consult user's manual if uncertain) Choose high pressure. Hold in the manual button and change setting to 8 (for 8 minutes).
3. Cook for 8 minutes. Turn off to release. Then open and remove the spaghetti squash.
4. Dig out the "noodles" with a spoon.
5. Stir the noodles in with your choice of sauce.
6. Dump the water out from the Instant Pot. Place the noodles back in and set to the warmer function. Warm up the noodles for one minute and serve.

Yellow Curry for Vegetarians

Prep time: 10 minutes

Cooking time: 6-8 hours

Ingredients:

- Three tablespoons olive oil
- Two cups butternut squash, cubed
- One cup soaked overnight, rinsed chickpeas
- One yellow onion, chopped
- Three cloves garlic, chopped
- Two cups coconut milk
- One cup chopped kale
- Two cups vegetable broth
- One tablespoon curcumin powder
- One tablespoon black pepper
- One tablespoon fenugreek
- One teaspoon chili powder
- One tablespoon garlic powder

Directions:

1. Place the ingredients in the instant pot.
2. Cook on the slow cook setting for 6-8 hours.
3. Serve over rice or noodles.

Deluxe and Delicious Potatoes

Prep time: 5-10 minutes

Cooking time: 6 hours (or while you are at work)

Ingredients:

- 5 large potatoes of your choice
- 2 tablespoons butter, warmed to liquid
- Two cups cheddar cheese
- One cup broccoli florets
- One teaspoon garlic powder
- One teaspoon black pepper
- 5 sheets of aluminum foil

Directions:

1. Poke the (unpeeled) potatoes with a fork. Dip them in the melted butter and wrap each one in tin foil.
1. Place in the Instant Pot.
2. Slow cook for 6-8 hours or while you are at work.
3. When you get home, remove the potatoes from the Instant Pot.
4. Slice the potatoes in half. Stuff with the cheddar cheese and broccoli and sprinkle with garlic powder and black pepper. Wrap them up again in the same tin foil.
5. Place the potatoes back in the Instant pot and warm for 5 minutes to melt the cheese.
6. Serve as is or with your favorite meat or fish dish.

Veggie Stuffed Peppers

Prep time: 5 minutes

Cooking time: 16 minutes

Ingredients:

- Four red bell peppers, tops cut off
- One cup white beans, soaked overnight
- One cup quinoa
- One cup goat cheese (chevre or feta)
- Three cups vegetable broth
- Two tablespoons garlic powder

Directions:

1. Place beans, quinoa, vegetable broth and garlic powder in the instant pot.

2. Cook on high pressure for 8 minutes.
3. Fill each pepper with the quinoa and bean mixture.
4. Wipe out the instant pot.
5. Place the filled peppers back in the instant pot and set instant pot to "warm" for 6 minutes.

Tofu, slow cooked

Prep time: 10 minutes

Cooking time: 6-8 hours

Ingredients:

- Three tablespoons olive oil
- Three tablespoons tamari sauce
- One tablespoon chopped ginger root
- Two cups tomato sauce
- ½ cup apple cider vinegar
- One tablespoon crushed red pepper
- One tablespoon black pepper
- One tablespoon garlic powder
- One tablespoon coconut sugar
- One zucchini, cubed
- ½ cup broccoli
- Two blocks medium firm tofu, cut into cubes

Directions:

1. Place all of the ingredients in the instant pot.
2. Cook on slow cook low heat for 6-8 hours.
3. Serve over rice or noodles.

Vegetarian Stroganoff

Prep time: 10 minutes

Cooking time: 6-8 hours

Ingredients:

- Three tablespoons olive oil
- Two cups mushrooms, sliced

- One red onion, diced
- Two cups vegetable broth
- One tablespoon paprika powder
- One tablespoon garlic powder
- Five cloves garlic, chopped
- Three tablespoons tamari
- One cup sour cream

Directions:

1. Place the ingredients in the instant pot.
2. Cook on the slow cook setting for 6-8 hours.
3. Serve over rice or noodles.

Spicy Quinoa Lentils

Prep time: 10 minutes

Cooking time: 6-8 hours

Ingredients:

- Three tablespoons olive oil
- Three cups vegetable broth
- One cup lentils, soaked and rinsed
- One cup quinoa, rinsed
- One cup tomato sauce
- Two tablespoons crushed red pepper
- Two tablespoons garlic powder
- Two garlic cloves, chopped
- ½ cup sun dried tomatoes

Directions:

1. Place the ingredients in the instant pot.
2. Cook on the slow cook setting for 6-8 hours.
3. Serve over rice or noodles.

Green Curry for Vegetarians

Prep time: 10 minutes

Cooking time: 6-8 hours

Ingredients:

- Three tablespoons olive oil
- One cup broccoli
- One green bell pepper, chopped
- Three tablespoons green curry seasoning
- Two cups coconut milk
- One cup vegetable broth
- One zucchini, sliced
- One carrot, chopped
- One handful fresh basil
- One tablespoon black pepper

Directions:

1. Place the ingredients in the instant pot.
2. Cook on the slow cook setting for 6-8 hours.
3. Serve over rice or noodles.

Celery Fennel Pot

Prep time: 10 minutes

Cooking time: 6-8 hours

Ingredients:

- Three tablespoons olive oil
- One celeriac, chopped
- Two stalks celery, chopped
- One bulb fennel, chopped
- One cup coconut cream
- One yellow onion, chopped
- Three cloves garlic, chopped
- Three cups vegetable broth
- One tablespoon curcumin powder
- One tablespoon black pepper
- One tablespoon garlic powder

Directions:

1. Place the ingredients in the instant pot.
2. Cook on the slow cook setting for 6-8 hours.
3. Serve over rice or noodles.

Root Vegetables

Prep time: 10 minutes

Cooking time: 6-8 hours

Ingredients:

- Three tablespoons olive oil
- One celeriac, chopped
- Two carrots, chopped
- One parsnip, chopped
- One rutabaga, diced
- One potato, cubed
- Three cloves garlic, chopped
- Three cups vegetable broth
- One tablespoon black pepper
- One tablespoon garlic powder

Directions:

1. Place the ingredients in the instant pot.
2. Cook on the slow cook setting for 6-8 hours.
3. Serve over rice or noodles.

Creamy Beans and Asparagus

Prep time: 10 minutes

Cooking time: 6-8 hours

Ingredients:

- Three tablespoons olive oil
- One cup green beans, cut into small pieces

- One cup white beans soaked and rinsed
- One cup asparagus, cut into bite-sized pieces
- One cup sour cream
- Three cloves garlic, chopped
- Three cups vegetable broth
- One tablespoon black pepper
- One tablespoon garlic powder

Directions:

1. Place the ingredients in the instant pot.
2. Cook on the slow cook setting for 6-8 hours.
3. Serve over rice or noodles.

Tomato Cream Cheese Pepper Stew

Prep time: 10 minutes

Cooking time: 6-8 hours

Ingredients:

- Three tablespoons olive oil
- One cup tomato sauce
- ½ cup cream cheese
- Two red bell peppers, chopped
- One yellow bell pepper, chopped
- One green bell pepper, chopped
- Three cloves garlic, chopped
- Two cups vegetable broth
- One tablespoon black pepper
- One tablespoon garlic powder

Directions:

1. Place the ingredients in the instant pot.
2. Cook on the slow cook setting for 6-8 hours.
3. Serve over rice or noodles.

Spicy Broccoli Potato

Prep time: 10 minutes

Cooking time: 6-8 hours

Ingredients:

- Three tablespoons olive oil
- Three cloves garlic, chopped
- Two cups broccoli florets
- Four potatoes, cubed
- One cup tomato sauce
- Two cups vegetable broth
- One cup sour cream
- One tablespoon black pepper
- One tablespoon garlic powder

Directions:

1. Place the ingredients in the instant pot.
2. Cook on the slow cook setting for 6-8 hours.
3. Serve over rice or noodles and optionally sprinkle with shredded cheddar cheese.

Fennel Cream

Prep time: 10 minutes

Cooking time: 6-8 hours

Ingredients:

- Three tablespoons olive oil
- Three bulbs fennel, chopped
- One potato, cubed
- One cup full fat cream
- Three cloves garlic, chopped
- Three cups vegetable broth
- One tablespoon black pepper
- One tablespoon garlic powder

Directions:

1. Place the ingredients in the instant pot.

2. Cook on the slow cook setting for 6-8 hours.
3. Serve over rice or noodles. Optionally sprinkle with swiss cheese.

Sweet potato Pumpkin Tofu Pot

Prep time: 10 minutes

Cooking time: 6-8 hours

Ingredients:

- Three tablespoons olive oil
- One block medium firm tofu
- One cup diced pumpkin
- Two sweet potatoes, peeled and chopped
- Three cloves garlic, chopped
- Three cups vegetable broth
- One tablespoon black pepper
- One tablespoon garlic powder

Directions:

1. Place the ingredients in the instant pot.
2. Cook on the slow cook setting for 6-8 hours.
3. Serve over rice or noodles.

Zucchini Carrot Garlic Noodles

Prep time: 10 minutes

Cooking time: 4 minutes

Ingredients:

- Three tablespoons olive oil
- Two cups (2-3 zucchini) spiralized
- Two cups spiralized carrots
- Three cloves garlic, chopped
- Two cups vegetable broth
- One tablespoon black pepper
- One tablespoon garlic powder

Directions:

1. Place the ingredients in the instant pot.
2. Cook on the high pressure setting for 4 minutes.
3. Allow pressure to release on its own and serve hot. Sprinkle with cheese if so desired.

Spicy Corn Potato Soup

Prep time: 10 minutes

Cooking time: 6-8 hours

Ingredients:

- Three tablespoons olive oil
- Four potatoes, cubed
- 2 cups sweet corn
- Three tablespoons crushed red pepper
- One tablespoon cornstarch
- Three cloves garlic, chopped
- Three cups vegetable broth
- One tablespoon black pepper
- One tablespoon garlic powder

Directions:

1. Place the ingredients in the instant pot.
2. Cook on the slow cook setting for 6-8 hours.
3. Serve over rice or noodles.

Creamy Coconut Onion Rutabaga

Prep time: 10 minutes

Cooking time: 6-8 hours

Ingredients:

- Two onions, sliced into rings
- One rutabaga, peeled and diced
- Three cloves garlic, chopped
- One cup vegetable broth
- Two cups coconut milk

- ½ cup coconut cream
- One tablespoon black pepper
- One tablespoon garlic powder

Directions:

1. Place the ingredients in the instant pot.
2. Cook on the slow cook setting for 6-8 hours.
3. Serve over rice or noodles.

Parsnip Gratin

Prep time: 10 minutes

Cooking time: 9 minutes

Ingredients:

- Three tablespoons olive oil
- Three cups (about five) parsnip, sliced
- Three cloves garlic, chopped
- Two cups vegetable broth
- One tablespoon black pepper
- One tablespoon garlic powder
- One cup cream cheese
- Two cups mozzarella cheese

Directions:

1. Place the ingredients in the instant pot, except for the mozzarella.
2. Cook on the high pressure setting for 4 minutes.
3. Allow pressure to release on its own. Top with the mozzarella cheese.
4. Set instant pot to warm for 5 minutes.
5. Serve and enjoy.

Sweet Potato Gratin

Prep time: 10 minutes

Cooking time: 9 minutes

Ingredients:

- Three tablespoons olive oil
- Four sweet potatoes, sliced into "coins"
- Three cloves garlic, chopped
- Two cups vegetable broth
- One teaspoon chili
- One tablespoon black pepper
- One tablespoon garlic powder
- One cup cream cheese
- Two cups cheddar cheese

Directions:

1. Place the ingredients in the instant pot, except for the cheddar.
2. Cook on the high pressure setting for 4 minutes.
3. Allow pressure to release on its own. Top with the cheddar cheese.
4. Set instant pot to warm for 5 minutes.
5. Serve and enjoy.

Zucchini Potato Casserole

Prep time: 10 minutes

Cooking time: 6-8 hours

Ingredients:

- Two zucchini, sliced into "coin" shapes
- Three potatoes, sliced into "coins"
- Three cloves garlic, chopped
- One cup vegetable broth
- Two cups coconut milk
- ½ cup coconut cream
- One tablespoon black pepper
- One tablespoon garlic powder

Directions:

1. Place the ingredients in the instant pot.
2. Cook on the slow cook setting for 6-8 hours.
3. Serve over rice or noodles.

Chapter 6: Soups and Stews

Creamy Corn Fish Soup

Prep time: 10 minutes

Cooking time: 6-8 hours

Ingredients:

- Two onions, sliced into rings
- One pound white fish without bones
- Two cups corn
- Three cloves garlic, chopped
- Two cups vegetable broth
- Two cups coconut milk
- ½ cup coconut cream
- One tablespoon black pepper
- One tablespoon garlic powder

Directions:

1. Place the ingredients in the instant pot.
2. Cook on the slow cook setting for 6-8 hours.
3. Serve with bread or salad.

Beef and Vegetable Stew

Prep time: 10 minutes

Cooking time: 1 hours

Ingredients:

- 2½ lb of beef, diced
- 1 cup of green peas
- 2 large onions, diced
- 1 lb of potatoes, diced
- 1 lb of carrots, diced
- 3 tbsp of oil
- 16 oz of chicken or vegetable stock
- 16 oz of tomato sauce
- ½ tsp of garlic powder

- 1 tsp of smoked paprika
- 1 tsp of kosher salt

Directions:
1. Brown the beef pieces in oil in cooking Pot on sauté setting.
2. Add salt while browning. Once meat is browned add chicken or vegetable stock, smoked paprika, and tomato sauce.
3. Set the timer to 15 minutes in soup mode.
4. Once timer beeps, add green peas, onions, carrots, potatoes, and garlic powder to the pot.
5. Cook on 'Soup Mode' setting for additional 30 minutes.

Pumpkin Soup

Prep time: 10 minutes

Cooking time: 12 minutes

Ingredients:

- 3 cups cubed hokkaido pumpkin
- 3 cups vegetable broth
- One cup coconut milk
- One onion, diced
- Three garlic cloves, chopped
- One pinch sea salt
- One teaspoon black pepper
- One teaspoon ginger powder
- Two tablespoons olive oil

Directions:
1. Set instant pot to saute. Add in olive oil, garlic, onion and pumpkin.
2. Put the rest of the remaining ingredients into the instant pot and stir.
3. Set to manual and cook for 10 minutes.
4. Allow the pressure to release on its own before opening.
5. Serve with good bread and/or salad.

Potato Soup

Prep time: 10 minutes

Cooking time: 12 minutes

Ingredients:

- 3 cups cubed potatoes (red potatoes are especially delicious)

- One yellow onion, diced
- Two cloves garlic, chopped
- One teaspoon black pepper
- One carrot, diced
- 3 cups vegetable broth (or chicken broth, if you prefer)

Directions:

1. Set instant pot to saute. Add in olive oil, garlic, onion and potatoes.
2. Put the rest of the remaining ingredients into the instant pot and stir.
3. Set to manual and cook for 10 minutes.
4. Allow the pressure to release on its own before opening.
5. Serve with good bread and/or salad.

Vegetable Soup

Prep time: 10 minutes

Cooking time: 12 minutes

Ingredients:

- 2 potatoes diced
- One yellow onion, diced
- Two cloves garlic, chopped
- One teaspoon black pepper
- One carrot, diced
- One cup diced celeriac
- One cup diced celery stalk
- ½ cup diced fennel
- 3 cups vegetable broth (or chicken broth, if you prefer)

Directions:

1. Set instant pot to saute. Add in olive oil, garlic, onion and potatoes.
2. Put the rest of the remaining ingredients into the instant pot and stir.
3. Set to manual and cook for 10 minutes.
4. Allow the pressure to release on its own before opening.
5. Serve with good bread and/or salad.

Warm Chicken Wrap

Prep time: 10 minutes

Cooking time: 10 minutes

Ingredients:

- 3 wraps (coconut wraps if on a low carb or gluten free diet)
- 1 ½ cups pepper jack cheese
- 3 tablespoons cream
- cheese
- One cup cooked chicken, shredded
- One large tomato, diced
- One handful baby spinach
- ½ cup grated carrots

Directions:

1. Spread a tablespoon of cream cheese on each of the wraps. Then add the chicken, tomato, spinach and carrots. Top with the mozzarella.
2. Place in the Instant Pot. Set to warmer function and then the timer to 8 minutes.
3. Serve with pickles and possibly a salad or soup.

Warm Meatball Sub

Prep time: 10 minutes

Cooking time: 12 minutes

Ingredients:

- 3 baguettes, sliced in half
- 3 cups meatballs (Italian or Swedish style)
- 2 cups tomato sauce
- 6 slices cheese

Directions:

1. Assemble each sub by arranging meatballs with tomato sauce and cheese.
2. Place in the Instant Pot and set to "warm". Warm for 8 minutes.
3. Enjoy.

Slow Cooked Chicken Chili

Prep time: 10 minutes

Cooking time: 6-8 hours

Ingredients:

- Four cups chicken broth from previous recipe (or another)
- 2 cups black beans
- One cup chopped tomatoes
- Two tablespoons tomato paste
- One teaspoon chili powder
- One teaspoon garlic powder
- ½ cup shredded chicken (can be from the chicken cooked in the previous recipe to make the chicken broth)
- Two tablespoons sour cream to top chili with
- One cup shredded cheese of your choice to top

Directions:

1. Place the chicken broth, beans, tomatoes, tomato paste, chili powder, garlic powder and chicken in the Instant Pot.
2. Set to slow cook setting for 6 hours. (The food will be kept warm even if you're not home to eat it).
3. When ready to eat, serve topped with the sour cream and shredded cheese.

Chicken Soup Broth

Prep time: 5 minutes

Cooking time: 30 minutes

Ingredients:

- One whole chicken or two breasts with bones
- 9 cups water
- One fennel stalk, chopped
- Two carrots, chopped
- One spring onion, chopped
- One celery root (celeriac), cubed and chopped
- One teaspoon whole or cracked peppercorns
- 4 cloves garlic, chopped
- ½ teaspoon sea salt

Directions:

1. Place the chicken and water in the Instant Pot along with the rest of the ingredients.
2. Use the high pressure setting to cook. Press in the manual button to add minutes for a total of 25 minutes.
3. Allow to sit for an addition 5-10 minutes. Serve as soup for lunch or use the broth in various other recipes.

Tomato Soup

Prep time: 10 minutes

Cooking time: 3-4 hours

Ingredients:

- Two onions, sliced into rings
- Two cups tomato sauce
- One handful fresh basil
- One cup sundried tomatoes
- Three cloves garlic, chopped
- Two cups vegetable broth
- One tablespoon black pepper
- One tablespoon garlic powder

Directions:

1. Place the ingredients in the instant pot.
2. Cook on the slow cook setting for 3-4 hours.
3. Serve over rice or noodles.

Carrot Ginger Soup

Prep time: 10 minutes

Cooking time: 6-8 hours

Ingredients:

- Five carrots, shredded
- One carrot, chopped
- One cup ginger, peeled and chopped
- Three cups vegetable broth
- One tablespoon black pepper
- One tablespoon garlic powder

Directions:

1. Place the ingredients in the instant pot.
2. Cook on the slow cook setting for 6-8 hours.
3. Use hand mixer to blend ingredients.
4. Serve hot with bread or salad.

Spicy Chicken Noodle Soup

Prep time: 10 minutes

Cooking time: 7 minutes

Ingredients:

- Two cups chicken, in bite sized pieces
- Five cups chicken stock
- One cup celery, chopped
- One celeriac root, cubed
- One potato, chopped
- One yellow onion, chopped
- One clove garlic, chopped
- One tablespoon black pepper
- One cup noodles, broken into smaller pieces

Directions:

1. Place the ingredients in the instant pot.
2. Set to high pressure setting and cook for 6 minutes.
3. Allow pressure to release on its own.

Beef Stew

Prep time: 10 minutes

Cooking time: 6-8 hours

Ingredients:

- Two large potatoes, chopped
- One cup beef tips, cut into bite-sized pieces
- One yellow onion, chopped
- One tablespoon cornstarch
- One cup celery, chopped
- One carrot, chopped

- Three cloves garlic, chopped
- Five cups beef broth
- One tablespoon black pepper
- One tablespoon garlic powder

Directions:

1. Place the ingredients in the instant pot.
2. Cook on the slow cook setting for 6-8 hours.
3. Serve with bread.

Bacon Broccoli Potato Soup

Prep time: 10 minutes

Cooking time: 6-8 hours

Ingredients:

- Two large potatoes, chopped
- One cup crispy bacon, torn into bite-sized pieces
- One yellow onion, chopped
- Two cups broccoli
- One tablespoon cornstarch
- One cup celery, chopped
- One carrot, chopped
- Three cloves garlic, chopped
- Five cups chicken broth
- One tablespoon black pepper
- One tablespoon garlic powder

Directions:

1. Place the ingredients in the instant pot.
2. Cook on the slow cook setting for 6-8 hours.
3. Serve with bread.

Thai Soup

Prep time: 10 minutes

Cooking time: 6-8 hours

Ingredients:

- Two large potatoes, chopped
- One cup chicken, cut into bite-sized pieces
- One yellow onion, chopped
- One tablespoon cornstarch
- One cup celery, chopped
- One carrot, chopped
- Three cloves garlic, chopped
- Five cups chicken broth
- Two cups coconut milk
- One cup coconut cream
- Two tablespoons curcumin
- Two tablespoons chili powder
- Two tablespoons lemongrass powder
- One tablespoon onion powder
- One tablespoon black pepper
- One tablespoon garlic powder

Directions:

1. Place the ingredients in the instant pot.
2. Cook on the slow cook setting for 6-8 hours.
3. Serve with bread and optionally top with soy sprouts.

Indian Stew

Prep time: 10 minutes

Cooking time: 6-8 hours

Ingredients:

- Three large potatoes, chopped
- Two cups chicken, cut into bite-sized pieces
- One yellow onion, chopped
- One tablespoon cornstarch
- One cup frozen spinach, thawed

- One carrot, chopped
- Three cloves garlic, chopped
- Five cups chicken broth
- Two cups coconut milk
- One cup coconut cream
- Two tablespoons curcumin
- Two tablespoons chili powder
- One tablespoon onion powder
- One tablespoon black pepper
- One tablespoon garlic powder

Directions:

1. Place the ingredients in the instant pot.
2. Cook on the slow cook setting for 6-8 hours.
3. Serve with bread and optionally top with soy sprouts.

Split Pea Soup

Prep time: 10 minutes

Cooking time: 6-8 hours

Ingredients:

- Three large potatoes, chopped
- 1 ½ cups dried peas, rinsed
- Two cups ham, cut into bite-sized pieces
- One yellow onion, chopped
- One carrot, chopped
- Three cloves garlic, chopped
- Five cups chicken broth
- One tablespoon onion powder
- One tablespoon black pepper
- One tablespoon garlic powder

Directions:

1. Place the ingredients in the instant pot.
2. Cook on the slow cook setting for 6-8 hours.
3. Serve with bread or salad.

Spicy Sausage Soup

Prep time: 10 minutes

Cooking time: 6-8 hours

Ingredients:

- Three large potatoes, chopped
- Three cups spicy sausage, sliced into bite-sized pieces
- One yellow onion, chopped
- One tablespoon cornstarch
- One cup black beans, rinsed and soaked overnight
- One carrot, chopped
- Three cloves garlic, chopped
- Six cups chicken broth
- Two tablespoons chili powder
- One tablespoon onion powder
- One tablespoon black pepper
- One tablespoon garlic powder

Directions:

1. Place the ingredients in the instant pot.
2. Cook on the slow cook setting for 6-8 hours.
3. Serve with bread and enjoy.

Deluxe Clam Chowder

Prep time: 10 minutes

Cooking time: 6-8 hours

Ingredients:

- Three large potatoes, chopped
- Two cups clams
- One cup clam juice
- Three cups vegetable stock
- Four cups whipping cream
- One yellow onion, chopped
- One tablespoon cornstarch
- One carrot, chopped
- Three cloves garlic, chopped

- One cup chicken broth
- One cup bacon
- One tablespoon onion powder
- One tablespoon black pepper
- One tablespoon garlic powder

Directions:

1. Place the ingredients in the instant pot.
2. Cook on the slow cook setting for 6-8 hours.
3. Serve with bread.

Chili Cheese Chicken Stew

Prep time: 10 minutes

Cooking time: 6-8 hours

Ingredients:

- Three large potatoes, chopped
- Two cups chicken, cut into bite-sized pieces
- One yellow onion, chopped
- One cup black beans, soaked and rinsed
- One carrot, chopped
- Three cloves garlic, chopped
- Seven cups chicken broth
- Two tablespoons chili powder
- One tablespoon onion powder
- One tablespoon black pepper
- One tablespoon garlic powder
- One cup cream cheese

Directions:

1. Place the ingredients in the instant pot.
2. Cook on the slow cook setting for 6-8 hours.
3. Serve with bread and top with cheddar cheese.

Cream of Celery Soup

Prep time: 10 minutes

Cooking time: 6-8 hours

Ingredients:

- Two celeriac roots, diced
- Three cups celery, chopped
- One yellow onion, chopped
- One carrot, chopped
- Three cloves garlic, chopped
- Seven cups vegetable broth
- One tablespoon onion powder
- One tablespoon black pepper
- One tablespoon garlic powder
- One cup cream cheese

Directions:

1. Place the ingredients in the instant pot.
2. Cook on the slow cook setting for 6-8 hours.
3. Serve with bread and top with cheddar cheese.

Dill Cream Potato Soup

Prep time: 10 minutes

Cooking time: 6-8 hours

Ingredients:

- Five potatoes, diced
- ½ cup fresh dill
- Three cups celery, chopped
- One yellow onion, chopped
- One carrot, chopped
- Three cloves garlic, chopped
- Seven cups vegetable broth
- One tablespoon onion powder
- One tablespoon black pepper
- One tablespoon garlic powder
- One cup cream cheese

Directions:

1. Place the ingredients in the instant pot.
2. Cook on the slow cook setting for 6-8 hours.
3. Serve with bread and optionally top with parmesan cheese.

Broccoli Bean Soup

Prep time: 10 minutes

Cooking time: 6-8 hours

Ingredients:

- Three large potatoes, chopped
- Two cups broccoli florets
- One yellow onion, chopped
- One cup black beans, soaked and rinsed
- One cup white beans, soaked and rinsed
- One carrot, chopped
- Three cloves garlic, chopped
- Seven cups chicken broth
- One tablespoon onion powder
- One tablespoon black pepper
- One tablespoon garlic powder

Directions:

1. Place the ingredients in the instant pot.
2. Cook on the slow cook setting for 6-8 hours.
3. Serve with bread.

Rice and Beef Soup

Prep time: 10 minutes

Cooking time: 6-8 hours

Ingredients:

- One cup rice

- Two cups beef tips
- One cup green beans
- One yellow onion, chopped
- One cup black beans, soaked and rinsed
- One cup white beans, soaked and rinsed
- One carrot, chopped
- Three cloves garlic, chopped
- Seven cups beef broth
- One tablespoon onion powder
- One tablespoon black pepper
- One tablespoon garlic powder

Directions:

1. Place the ingredients in the instant pot.
2. Cook on the slow cook setting for 6-8 hours.
3. Serve with bread.

Spicy Vegetable Soup

Prep time: 10 minutes

Cooking time: 6-8 hours

Ingredients:

- Three large potatoes, chopped
- Two cups broccoli florets
- One yellow onion, chopped
- ½ cup chopped sundried tomatoes
- One carrot, chopped
- One parsnip, chopped
- One diced celeriac root
- One cup chopped celery
- Three cloves garlic, chopped
- Three tablespoons crushed red pepper
- Seven cups vegetable broth
- One tablespoon onion powder
- One tablespoon black pepper
- One tablespoon garlic powder

Directions:

1. Place the ingredients in the instant pot.
2. Cook on the slow cook setting for 6-8 hours.
3. Serve with bread.

Pumpkin Rice Soup

Prep time: 10 minutes

Cooking time: 6-8 hours

Ingredients:

- One cup rice
- Two cups broccoli florets
- One yellow onion, chopped
- Two cups hokkaido pumpkin
- One carrot, chopped
- Three cloves garlic, chopped
- Five cups vegetable broth
- One cup coconut milk
- One tablespoon coconut oil
- One tablespoon onion powder
- One tablespoon black pepper
- One tablespoon garlic powder

Directions:

1. Place the ingredients in the instant pot.
2. Cook on the slow cook setting for 6-8 hours.
3. Serve with bread.

Pumpkin Noodle Soup

Prep time: 10 minutes

Cooking time: 6-8 hours

Ingredients:

- One cup soy noodles
- One yellow onion, chopped
- Two cups hokkaido pumpkin
- One carrot, chopped

- Three cloves garlic, chopped
- Five cups chicken broth
- One cup coconut milk
- One tablespoon coconut oil
- One tablespoon onion powder
- Two tablespoons black pepper
- One tablespoon garlic powder
- Two tablespoons ginger powder

Directions:

1. Place the ingredients in the instant pot.
2. Cook on the slow cook setting for 6-8 hours.
3. Serve with bread.

Quinoa Black Bean Beef Soup

Prep time: 10 minutes

Cooking time: 6-8 hours

Ingredients:

- One cup quinoa, rinsed well
- One cups broccoli florets
- One cup beef steak tips
- One yellow onion, chopped
- One cup black beans, soaked overnight and rinsed
- One carrot, chopped
- Three cloves garlic, chopped
- Five cups vegetable broth
- One cup coconut milk
- One tablespoon coconut oil
- One tablespoon onion powder
- One tablespoon black pepper
- One tablespoon garlic powder
- Two tablespoons ginger powder

Directions:

1. Place the ingredients in the instant pot.
2. Cook on the slow cook setting for 6-8 hours.
3. Serve with bread.

Beans and Grains

Prep time: 2 minutes

Cooking time: 5 minutes

Ingredients:

- One cup quinoa
- 1 ½ cups water
- ½ cup feta cheese
- One pinch sea salt

Directions:

1. Place water and quinoa in instant pot.
2. Cook on high pressure for 2 minutes. Allow pressure to release on its own.
3. Open and add sea salt and feta cheese.
4. Serve as a side to your favorite warm meal or salad.

Black Bean Onion

Prep time: 5 minutes

Cooking time: 6-8 hours

Ingredients:

- One cup black beans soaked and rinsed
- Two cups water
- One onion, chopped
- One pinch sea salt.

Directions:

1. Place the ingredients in the instant pot.
2. Cook on the slow cook setting for 6-8 hours.
3. Serve as a delicious side dish.

Chickpeas and Tomatoes

Prep time: 10 minutes

Cooking time: 6-8 hours

Ingredients:

- One cup chickpeas, rinsed and soaked
- Two cups water
- One tomato, chopped

Directions:

1. Place the ingredients in the instant pot.
2. Cook on the slow cook setting for 6-8 hours.
3. Serve as a side dish.

Maple Brown Rice

Prep time: 5 minutes

Cooking time: 10 minutes

Ingredients:

- One cup brown rice
- 1 ½ cups water
- Two tablespoons maple syrup

Directions:

1. Place the ingredients in the instant pot.
2. Set to high pressure and cook for 8 minutes.
3. Allow pressure to release naturally.

Wild Rice and Goat Cheese

Prep time: 5 minutes

Cooking time: 10 minutes

Ingredients:

- One cup
- One ½ cups water
- Two tablespoons chevre

Directions:

1. Place the rice and water in the instant pot.
2. Set to high pressure and cook for 8 minutes.
3. Allow pressure to release naturally.
4. Add in the goat cheese.

Rice and Carrots Side Dish

Prep time: 5 minutes

Cooking time: 10 minutes

Ingredients:

- One cup white rice
- 1 ½ cups water
- one carrot, shredded

Directions:

1. Place the ingredients in the instant pot.
2. Set to high pressure and cook for 8 minutes.
3. Allow pressure to release naturally.

Stewed Pea Side Dish

Prep time: 5 minutes

Cooking time: 6 hours

Ingredients:

- Two cups freeze dried peas
- Three cups chicken stock
- ½ cup cubed ham bits

Directions:

1. Place the ingredients in the instant pot.
2. Cook on low heat (slow cooker mode) for 6 hours.
3. Serve alongside your favorite dish.

Beans and Bacon

Prep time: 5 minutes

Cooking time: 6 hours

Ingredients:

- One cup black beans, soaked and rinsed
- 1 ½ cups water
- ½ cup bacon bits

Directions:

1. Place the ingredients in the instant pot.
2. Slow cook for six hours.
3. Serve as a side dish to your favorite meals.

Chicken Carrot Rice

Prep time: 5 minutes

Cooking time: 10 minutes

Ingredients:

- 1 ½ cups brown rice
- 2 cups chicken broth
- One carrot, chopped

Directions:

1. Place the ingredients in the instant pot.
2. Set to high pressure and cook for 8 minutes.
3. Allow pressure to release naturally.

Kidney Bean Beef Side Dish

Prep time: 5 minutes

Cooking time: 10 minutes

Ingredients:

- One cup kidney beans, soaked and rinsed
- 1 ½ cups beef broth

Directions:

1. Place the ingredients in the instant pot.
2. Set to high pressure and cook for 8 minutes.
3. Allow pressure to release naturally.

Millet Garlic Side Dish

Prep time: 5 minutes

Cooking time: 10 minutes

Ingredients:

- One cup millet
- 1 ½ cups water
- Two tablespoons garlic powder

Directions:

1. Place the ingredients in the instant pot.
2. Set to high pressure and cook for 8 minutes.
3. Allow pressure to release naturally.

Bulgur Broccoli

Prep time: 5 minutes

Cooking time: 10 minutes

Ingredients:

- One cup bulgur
- 1 ½ cups vegetable stock
- ½ cup broccoli florets

Directions:

1. Place the ingredients in the instant pot.
2. Set to high pressure and cook for 8 minutes.
3. Allow pressure to release naturally.

Couscous Tomato

Prep time: 5 minutes

Cooking time: 10 minutes

Ingredients:

- One cup couscous
- 1 ½ cups water
- One tomato, chopped
- One pinch sea salt

Directions:

1. Place the ingredients in the instant pot.
2. Set to high pressure and cook for 8 minutes.
3. Allow pressure to release naturally.

Cream Cheese Amaranth

Prep time: 5 minutes

Cooking time: 10 minutes

Ingredients:

- One cup amaranth
- 1 ½ cups water
- Two tablespoons cream cheese

Directions:

1. Place the ingredients (except for the cream cheese) in the instant pot.
2. Set to high pressure and cook for 8 minutes.
3. Allow pressure to release naturally.
4. Add in the cream cheese.
5. Serve as a side alongside your favorite meals.

Quinoa Kale

Prep time: 5 minutes

Cooking time: 10 minutes

Ingredients:

- One cup quinoa
- 1 ½ cups water
- One cup chopped kale
- One tablespoon garlic salt

Directions:

1. Place the ingredients in the instant pot.
2. Set to high pressure and cook for 8 minutes.
3. Allow pressure to release naturally.

Quinoa Rice Medley

Prep time: 5 minutes

Cooking time: 10 minutes

Ingredients:

- ½ cup brown rice
- ½ cup quinoa
- 1 ½ cups water

Directions:

1. Place the ingredients in the instant pot.
2. Set to high pressure and cook for 8 minutes.
3. Allow pressure to release naturally.

Black Bean Sweet Potato Side

Prep time: 5 minutes

Cooking time: 10 minutes

Ingredients:

- One cup black beans, soaked and rinsed
- ½ cup sweet potatoes, cubed
- 1 ½ cups water
- One tablespoon garlic powder

Directions:

1. Place the ingredients in the instant pot.
2. Set to high pressure and cook for 8 minutes.
3. Allow pressure to release naturally.

Giant Bean Sweet Onion Side

Prep time: 5 minutes

Cooking time: 10 minutes

Ingredients:

- One cup giant beans, soaked and rinsed
- 1 ½ cups water
- One sweet onion, chopped

Directions:

1. Place the ingredients in the instant pot.
2. Set to high pressure and cook for 8 minutes.
3. Allow pressure to release naturally.

Spelt rice

Prep time: 5 minutes

Cooking time: 10 minutes

Ingredients:

- One cup spelt
- 1 ½ cups vegetable broth

Directions:

1. Place the ingredients in the instant pot.
2. Set to high pressure and cook for 8 minutes.
3. Allow pressure to release naturally.

Spelt rice and garlic butter

Prep time: 5 minutes

Cooking time: 10 minutes

Ingredients:

- One cup spelt
- 1 ½ cups vegetable broth
- One tablespoon butter
- One tablespoon garlic powder

Directions:

1. Place the ingredients in the instant pot.
2. Set to high pressure and cook for 8 minutes.
3. Allow pressure to release naturally.

Chapter 7: Snacks

Apple Cherry Sauce

Prep time: 5-10 minutes

Cooking time: 6-8 hours or while you are at work Ingredients

Ingredients:

- 4 pounds of apples (about 8 large apples)
- One tablespoon of cinnamon (or cook with a cinnamon stick)
- 1 cup water
- Two cups cherries with the seeds removed

Directions:

1. Peel and chop the apples.
2. Place all of the ingredients in the Instant Pot. Set to slow cooker setting and cook for 6 hours.
3. Serve when ready as a snack or top with maple syrup, cream or ice cream as a dessert.

Coconut Sugar Cashews

Prep time: 5 minutes

Cooking time: 4 hours

Ingredients:

- 3 cups cashews
- One cup coconut sugar
- 4 tablespoons coconut oil
- One egg, beaten
- Three tablespoons almond flour

Directions:

1. Mix the ingredients in a mixing bowl.
2. Transfer to the Instant Pot. Set for slow cooker and press in the "manual" button to select 4 hours.
3. Cook for 4 hours. Serve warm and serve for guests or top ice cream with the cashews for an extra special dessert treat.

Maple Carrots

Prep time: 5 minutes

Cooking time: 4 hours

Ingredients:

- 3 cups carrots, cut into sticks (or very small carrots)
- 4 tablespoons maple syrup
- 4 tablespoons coconut oil

Directions:

1. Mix the ingredients in a mixing bowl.
2. Transfer to the Instant Pot. Set for slow cooker and press in the "manual" button to select 4 hours.
3. Enjoy as a healthy and sweet snack.

Sausage Cheese Dip

Prep time: 5 minutes

Cooking time: 5 minutes

Ingredients:

- One cup spicy sausage (kielbasa is a good choice)
- Two cups cream cheese
- One beaten egg
- Two cups pepper jack cheese

Directions:

1. Mix the ingredients in a mixing bowl.
2. Transfer to the Instant Pot. Set pressure cooker setting to high and set the timer for 5 minutes.
3. Serve with chips or vegetables (celery, raw carrot sticks, raw broccoli, etc).

Pizza Dip

Prep time: 5 minutes

Cooking time: 5 minutes

Ingredients:

- Three cups marinara or pizza sauce
- Three cups cream cheese
- One beaten egg
- One teaspoon garlic powder
- Four cups shredded mozzarella cheese
- Optional pepperoni

Directions:

1. Mix the egg, cream cheese and garlic powder in a mixing bowl.
2. Spoon the egg and cream cheese mixture into the Instant Pot.
3. Add the pizza sauce and then top with the mozzarella cheese and finally the pepperoni.
4. High pressure cook for five minutes. Serve with tortilla chips or bread sticks.

Melted Cheese Wrap

Prep time: 5 minutes

Cooking time: 8 minutes

Ingredients:

- 3 wraps (coconut wraps if on a low carb or gluten free diet)
- 1 ½ cups mozzarella cheese
- 3 tablespoons cream cheese
- One large tomato, diced
- One handful baby spinach
- ½ cup grated carrots

Directions:

1. Spread a tablespoon of cream cheese on each of the wraps. Then add the tomato, spinach and carrots. Top with the mozzarella.
2. Place in the Instant Pot. Set to warmer function and then the timer to 8 minutes.
3. Serve with pickles and possibly a salad or soup.

Maple Cashews

Prep time: 5 minutes

Cooking time: 2-3 hours

Ingredients:

- Two cups cashews
- One cup maple syrup
- One pinch cinnamon
- One pinch salt

Directions:

1. Combine all the ingredients in a bowl.
2. Transfer to the Instant pot. Cook on slow cooker setting for 2-3 hours.
3. Allow the cashews to cool before enjoying.

Chex Trail Mix

Prep time: 5 minutes

Cooking time: 2-3 hours

Ingredients:

- One cup cashews
- One cup chex (or other crunchy cereal)
- One cup craisins (or comparable dried cranberries)
- One cup maple syrup or coconut nectar
- ½ cup peanuts
- ½ cup pretzel sticks
- One pinch cinnamon
- One dash vanilla extract

Directions:

1. Combine all the ingredients in a bowl.
2. Transfer to the Instant pot. Cook on slow cooker setting for 2-3 hours.
3. Allow the trail mix to cool down before enjoying on a hike or for whatever occasion you choose.

Cream Cheese Spinach Dip

Prep time: 5 minutes

Cooking time: 2-3 hours

Ingredients:

- Three cups cream cheese
- One cup scallions
- One cup baby spinach
- Two cups mozzarella cheese

Directions:

1. Combine all the ingredients in a bowl.
2. Transfer to the Instant pot. Cook on slow cooker setting for 2-3 hours.
3. Serve with chips or veggies.

Mexican Pizza Dip

Prep time: 5 minutes

Cooking time: 2-3 hours

Ingredients:

- Three cups sour cream
- Three cups salsa
- Three cups pepper jack or other spicy cheese

Directions:

1. Place the sour cream in the instant pot.
2. Then layer on the salsa. Then top with the cheese.
3. Allow to cook for 2-3 hours before serving with tortilla chips or vegetables.

Cream Cheese Tomatoes

Prep time: 5 minutes

Cooking time: 2-3 hours

Ingredients:

- One cup cream cheese
- Four large tomatoes, insides removed

- One teaspoon garlic powder

Directions:

1. Combine the cream cheese and garlic powder in a bowl.
2. Scoop the cream cheese into the tomatoes.
3. Place in the instant pot and cook as indicated, on the slow cook setting for 2 hours.

Chapter 8: Sauces

Tomato Sauce

Prep time: 5 minutes

Cooking time: 6-8 hours

Ingredients:

- Two cups tomato paste
- Two tomatoes, chopped
- One cup sun dried tomatoes, chopped
- ½ cup apple cider vinegar
- One tablespoon honey
- Three cloves garlic, chopped
- One onion chopped.

Directions:

1. Place the ingredients in the instant pot.
2. Slow cook for 6-8 hours.
3. Serve with pasta or rice.

Perfect cheese sauce

Prep time: 5 minutes

Cooking time: 8 minutes

Ingredients:

- One cup chicken broth
- One cup cream cheese
- Two cups cheddar cheese
- One tablespoon garlic powder

Directions:

1. Place the ingredients in the instant pot.
2. Use the "warm" setting and warm for 8 minutes.

3. Serve with chips, vegetables or as a sauce for noodles.

Broccoli Cream Sauce

Prep time: 5 minutes

Cooking time: 8 minutes

Ingredients:

- One cup chicken broth
- One cup cream cheese
- Two cups cheddar cheese
- One tablespoon garlic powder
- One cup broccoli
- One tablespoon black pepper

Directions:

1. Place the ingredients in the instant pot.
2. Use the "warm" setting and warm for 8 minutes.
3. Serve with chips, vegetables or as a sauce for noodles.

Coconut Carrot Sauce

Prep time: 5 minutes

Cooking time: 8 minutes

Ingredients:

- One cup coconut milk
- One cup cream cheese
- Two cups swiss cheese
- One tablespoon garlic powder
- One shredded carrots
- One tablespoon black pepper

Directions:

1. Place the ingredients in the instant pot.
2. Use the "warm" setting and warm for 8 minutes.

3. Serve with chips, vegetables or as a sauce for noodles.

Cream Cheese and Chives Sauce

Prep time: 5 minutes

Cooking time: 8 minutes

Ingredients:

- One cup chicken broth
- One cup cream cheese
- Two cups swiss cheese
- ½ cup chopped scallions

Directions:

1. Place the ingredients in the instant pot.
2. Use the "warm" setting and warm for 8 minutes.
3. Serve with chips, vegetables or as a sauce for noodles.

Onion Sauce

Prep time: 5 minutes

Cooking time: 8 minutes

Ingredients:

- One cup vegetable broth
- Two cups cream cheese
- Two tablespoons onion powder
- One chopped yellow onion

Directions:

1. Place the ingredients in the instant pot.
2. Use the "warm" setting and warm for 8 minutes.
3. Serve with chips, vegetables or as a sauce for noodles.

Pepper Sauce

Prep time: 5 minutes

Cooking time: 6-8 hours

Ingredients:

- One cup vegetable broth
- Two cups chopped red bell pepper
- One tablespoon paprika
- One cup sun dried tomatoes, chopped
- ½ cup apple cider vinegar
- One tablespoon honey
- Three cloves garlic, chopped
- One onion chopped.

Directions:

1. Place the ingredients in the instant pot.
2. Slow cook for 6-8 hours.
3. Serve with pasta or rice.

Parmesan Basil Sauce

Prep time: 5 minutes

Cooking time: 10 minutes

Ingredients:

- One cup cream cheese
- Two tablespoons olive oil
- Two cups fresh basil, chopped
- One tablespoon parmesan
- One tablespoon black pepper

Directions:

1. Place the ingredients in the instant pot.
2. Pressure cook on low for 5 minutes.
3. Serve with pasta or rice.

Goat cheese and tomato sauce

Prep time: 5 minutes

Cooking time: 10 minutes

Ingredients:

- Two cups tomato paste
- Two tomatoes, chopped
- One cup sun dried tomatoes, chopped
- ½ cup apple cider vinegar
- One tablespoon honey
- Three cloves garlic, chopped
- One onion chopped
- One cup goat cheese
- One tablespoon parmesan cheese
- ½ cup mozzarella cheese

Directions:

1. Place the ingredients in the instant pot.
2. Slow cook for 6-8 hours.
3. Serve with pasta or rice.

Buttery Coconut Sauce

Prep time: 5 minutes

Cooking time: 10 minutes

Ingredients:

- One cup melted butter
- One cup coconut cream
- One tablespoon garlic powder

Directions:

1. Place the ingredients in the instant pot.
2. Cook on the "warm" mode setting for 8 minutes.

Chapter 9: Desserts

Maple bread pudding

Prep time: 5 minutes

Cooking time: 10 minutes

Ingredients:

- One cup melted butter
- 7 pieces of bread
- One cup maple syrup
- 4 eggs
- One cup whipping cream
- One teaspoon vanilla extract

Directions:

1. Grease an oven safe form that fits in your instant pot with the butter
2. Combine the syrup, eggs, cream and vanilla.
3. Place the bread in the instant pot and pour the cream mixture over it.
4. Cover with tin foil.
5. Set instant pot to high pressure and adjust valve to manual.
6. Cook for 12 minutes and allow pressure to release on its own.
7. Serve with vanilla ice cream.

Apple bread pudding

Prep time: 5 minutes

Cooking time: 10 minutes

Ingredients:

- One cup melted butter
- 8 pieces of bread
- One cup maple syrup
- 5 eggs
- One cup whipping cream
- One teaspoon vanilla extract
- One tablespoon cinnamon
- One cup apple sauce

Directions:

1. Grease an oven safe form that fits in your instant pot with the butter
2. Combine the syrup, eggs, cream, cinnamon, apple sauce and vanilla.
3. Place the bread in the instant pot and pour the cream mixture over it.
4. Cover with tin foil.
5. Set instant pot to high pressure and adjust valve to manual.
6. Cook for 12 minutes and allow pressure to release on its own.
7. Serve with vanilla ice cream.

Maple Almond Rice Pudding

Prep time: 5 minutes

Cooking time: 10 minutes

Ingredients:

- One cup melted butter
- One cup heavy cream
- 1 ½ cups water
- One teaspoon almond extract
- One cup maple syrup
- One cup instant rice
- Two eggs
- ½ teaspoon vanilla extract
- One tablespoon coconut nectar

Directions:

1. Fill your instant pot with all of the ingredients.
2. Stir well.
3. Slow cook on the slow cook setting for 6-8 hours.
4. Serve warm or chill in refrigerator.
5. Top with whipped cream and fresh fruit such as strawberries. Garnish with a sprig of mint.

Strawberries and millet cream pudding

Prep time: 5 minutes

Cooking time: 10 minutes

Ingredients:

- One cup melted butter
- Two cups heavy cream
- 1 cup water
- One teaspoon vanilla extract
- One cup frozen and thawed strawberries
- One egg
- One cup maple syrup
- One cup millet flakes

Directions:

1. Fill your instant pot with all of the ingredients.
2. Stir well.
3. Slow cook on the slow cook setting for 6-8 hours.
4. Serve warm or chill in refrigerator.
5. Top with whipped cream and fresh fruit such as strawberries. Garnish with a sprig of mint.

Banana Bread Pudding

Prep time: 5 minutes

Cooking time: 12 minutes

Ingredients:

- One cup melted butter
- 7 pieces of bread
- One cup maple syrup
- 4 eggs
- 3 bananas, mashed
- One cup coconut cream
- One teaspoon vanilla extract

Directions:

1. Grease an oven safe form that fits in your instant pot with the butter
2. Combine the syrup, eggs, banana, cream and vanilla.
3. Place the bread in the instant pot and pour the cream mixture over it.
4. Cover with tin foil.
5. Set instant pot to high pressure and adjust valve to manual.
6. Cook for 12 minutes and allow pressure to release on its own.
7. Serve with vanilla ice cream.

Apple Crisp

Prep time: 5 minutes

Cooking time: 6-8 hours

Ingredients:

- One cup melted butter
- Two cups brown sugar or coconut sugar
- Two cups steel cut oats
- One teaspoon vanilla extract
- One egg
- Seven peeled and sliced apples
- Two tablespoons cinnamon

Directions:

1. Fill your instant pot with all of the ingredients.
2. Stir well.
3. Slow cook on the slow cook setting for 6-8 hours.
4. Serve warm.
5. Top with vanilla ice cream

Chocolate Peanut Butter Pudding

Prep time: 5 minutes

Cooking time: 6-8 hours

Ingredients:

- One cup melted butter
- Three cups maple syrup
- Four eggs

- Two cups whipping cream
- Three tablespoons cocoa powder
- Two tablespoons peanut butter
- One tablespoon cornstarch

Directions:

1. Fill your instant pot with all of the ingredients.
2. Stir well.
3. Slow cook on the slow cook setting for 6-8 hours.
4. Serve warm or chill in refrigerator.
5. Top with vanilla ice cream

Apple Cheesecake

Prep time: 5 minutes

Cooking time: 10 minutes

Ingredients:

- ½ cup applesauce
- Four cups cream cheese
- 3 eggs
- One teaspoon vanilla extract

Directions:

1. Grease a pie pan that fits in the instant pot with butter or coconut oil.
2. Mix the applesauce with the cream cheese, eggs and vanilla.
3. Place in the pie pan.
4. Cook on high pressure for 10 minutes. Allow pressure valve to release on its own.
5. Allow to cool and serve with cream or top with cherries and apples.

Berry Crisp

Prep time: 5 minutes

Cooking time: 6-8 hours

Ingredients:

- One cup melted butter

- Two cups brown sugar or coconut sugar
- Two cups steel cut oats
- One teaspoon vanilla extract
- Three cups raspberries, blueberries and strawberries (frozen and thawed)
- One tablespoon almond butter

Directions:

1. Fill your instant pot with all of the ingredients.
2. Stir well.
3. Slow cook on the slow cook setting for 6-8 hours.
4. Serve warm.
5. Top with vanilla ice cream

Sweet Zucchini Bread

Prep time: 5 minutes

Cooking time: 18 minutes

Ingredients:

- One cup melted butter
- Two cups brown sugar or coconut sugar
- Two cups flour
- Two zucchini, shredded
- One cup applesauce
- Two eggs
- ½ cup heavy cream
- One teaspoon baking powder

Directions:

1. Mix the ingredients well.
2. Grease a bread pan with coconut oil or butter.
3. Pour the batter into the pan.
4. Cover with tin foil.
5. Pour a cup of water into the instant pot.
6. Place the bread pan into the instant pot and cook for 18 minutes on high pressure.
7. Serve topped with butter or even ice cream.

Chocolate Rice Pudding

Prep time: 5 minutes

Cooking time: 25 minutes

Ingredients:
- One cup rice
- 5 cups coconut milk (or 1% milk)
- One teaspoon vanilla extract
- Two tablespoons cocoa powder
- One cup coconut sugar
- One tablespoon coconut oil
- Two eggs, beaten

Directions:
1. Place all of the ingredients in the Instant Pot and press sautee.
2. Stir constantly and bring to a boil.
3. Cover and seal and press "rice" button.
4. When rice program is finished, turn off and allow to sit for 15 minutes. Stir and serve topped with raspberries or heavy cream.

Vanilla Rice Pudding

Prep time: 5 minutes

Cooking time: 8 minutes

Ingredients:

- Two cups rice flour
- 4 cups coconut milk (or rice milk)
- Two teaspoons vanilla extract
- One cup coconut nectar (syrup)
- One tablespoon coconut oil

Directions:

1. Place all of the ingredients in the Instant Pot. Stir well to distribute the ingredients evenly.
2. Cook high pressure for 7 minutes. Allow to stand for 5 and stir well.
3. Serve topped with cherries or your choice of topping.

Cherry Cheesecake

Prep time: 8 minutes

Cooking time: 40 minutes

Ingredients:

- 4 cups softened cream cheese
- One tablespoon heavy cream
- 3 eggs, beaten
- One teaspoon vanilla extract
- One prepared crust, or cake pan greased with coconut oil if going crust free

Directions:

1. Blend ingredients well in a food processor or by hand. (A high speed blender such as vita mix can also be used)
2. Place the cake mixture into the pre-greased pan. Wrap in parchment paper and then with tin foil.
3. Place two cups of water into the Instant Pot.
4. Set on high pressure and turn the lever to "sealing".
5. Adjust to cook for 40 minutes. Allow to release and cool before removing.
6. Top with cherries, strawberry jam, chocolate or other choice of topping.

Peanut Butter Brownies

Prep time: 5 minutes

Cooking time: 12 minutes

Ingredients:

- Two tablespoons coconut oil
- One cup cream cheese
- Two tablespoons peanut butter
- 1 ½ cups peanut flour
- ½ cup cocoa powder
- 3 eggs, beaten

Directions:

1. Mix all the ingredients in a mixing bowl with a hand mixer (food processor may also be used).
2. Place the ingredients in an oven safe form. Wrap the form with tin foil.
3. Place two cups of water in the Instant Pot.
4. Cook on high pressure (sealed) for 12 minutes.

5. Serve with ice cream or whipped cream.

Sticky Date and Pears

Prep time: 5 minutes

Cooking time: 4 hours

Ingredients:

- Three cups peeled and chopped pears
- One cup chopped dates
- One teaspoon vanilla extract
- One cup water
- One tablespoon maple syrup

Directions:

1. Place all the ingredients in the Instant Pot.
2. Set to slow cooker and cook for four hours. Serve topped with whipped cream or allow to chill and even eat for breakfast.

Cream Cheese Honey Fruit Dip

Prep time: 5 minutes

Cooking time: 2-3 hours

Ingredients:

- Three cups cream cheese
- Two tablespoons cream
- ½ cup honey

Directions:

1. Combine all the ingredients in a bowl.
2. Transfer to the Instant pot. Cook on slow cooker setting for 2-3 hours.
3. Serve as a dip for fruit or cookies or biscuits. Strawberries and bananas are especially perfect for this dessert.

Chocolate Fruit Dip

Prep time: 5 minutes

Cooking time: 2-3 hours

Ingredients:

- One cup sour cream
- ½ cup full fat cream
- Three tablespoons cocoa powder
- One teaspoon vanilla extract
- Three tablespoons cashew butter
- ½ cup coconut nectar

Directions:

1. Combine all the ingredients in a bowl.
2. Transfer to the Instant pot. Cook on slow cooker setting for 2-3 hours.
3. Serve as a dip for fruit or cookies or biscuits. Strawberries and bananas are especially perfect for this dessert.

Peanut Butter Chocolate Cake

Prep time: 5 minutes

Cooking time: 2-3 hours

Ingredients:

- One cup white flour
- ½ cup sugar
- 3 tablespoons cocoa powder
- One teaspoon baking powder
- 3 tablespoons coconut oil, warmed to room temperature
- One tablespoon vanilla extract
- 3 tablespoons peanut butter
- One additional tablespoon coconut oil
- ½ cup coconut milk
- One egg

Directions:

1. Grease the inside of the instant pot with the tablespoon of coconut oil.
2. Combine the rest of the ingredients in a large mixing bowl until smooth.
3. Pour into instant pot and slow cook for two to three hours. Check progress by sticking a fork or skewer into the cake. If it comes out clean, your cake is ready.

4. Allow to cool slightly and serve ideally with vanilla ice cream.

Whole Grain Fruit Cake

Prep time: 5 minutes

Cooking time: 2-3 hours

Ingredients:

- One cup whole wheat flour
- ½ cup sugar
- One teaspoon baking powder
- 3 tablespoons coconut oil, warmed to room temperature
- One tablespoon vanilla extract
- One additional tablespoon coconut oil
- ½ cup cream
- One egg
- One cup chopped apples

Directions:

1. Grease the inside of the instant pot with the tablespoon of coconut oil.
2. Combine the rest of the ingredients in a large mixing bowl until smooth.
3. Pour into instant pot and slow cook for two to three hours. Check progress by sticking a fork or skewer into the cake. If it comes out clean, your cake is ready.
4. Allow to cool slightly and serve ideally with vanilla ice cream.

Warm Cherry Fruit

Prep time: 5 minutes

Cooking time: 2-3 hours

Ingredients:

- One cup cherries, pits removed
- One cup raspberries
- One cup apples, peeled and chopped into pieces
- One cup honey

Directions:

1. Place the ingredients in the instant pot. Stir.
2. Slow cook for about three hours. Stir and serve over ice cream, cake or pudding.

Nutrition Tables

Vegetables

3 oz of food	Calories	Fat	Protein	Carbs	Fiber
Pecans	691	72g	9g	14g	10g
Walnuts	654	65g	15g	14g	7g
Hazelnuts	628	61g	15g	17g	10g
Sunflower Seeds	584	51g	21g	20g	9g
Almonds	575	49g	21g	22g	12g
Sesame Seeds	573	50g	18g	23g	12g
Pumpkin Seeds	541	46g	25g	18g	4g
Soybeans	446	20g	36g	30g	9g
Quinoa	368	6g	14g	64g	7g
Beans, Pinto	347	1g	21g	63g	15g
Black Beans	341	1g	22g	62g	15g
Beans, Kidney	337	1g	23g	61g	15g
Beans, Navy	337	1g	22g	61g	24g
Cranberry Beans	335	1g	23g	60g	25g
Mushrooms, Shiitake	296	1g	10g	75g	11g
Avocado	160	15g	2g	9g	7g
Garlic	149	0g	6g	33g	2g
Yams	118	0g	2g	28g	4g
Bananas	89	0g	1g	23g	3g
Corn	86	1g	3g	19g	3g
Sweet Potato	86	0g	2g	20g	3g
Pomegranates	83	1g	2g	19g	4g
Peas	81	0g	5g	14g	5g
Potatoes, Russet	79	0g	2g	18g	1g
Parsnips	75	0g	1g	18g	5g
Figs	74	0g	1g	19g	3g
Shallots	72	0g	3g	17g	0g
Kumquats	71	1g	2g	16g	6g
Potatoes, Red	70	0g	2g	16g	2g
Guava	68	1g	3g	14g	5g
Grapes	67	0g	1g	17g	1g
Cherries	63	0g	1g	16g	2g
Leeks	61	0g	1g	14g	2g
Pears	58	0g	0g	15g	3g

Blueberries	57	0g	1g	14g	2g
Tangerines	53	0g	1g	13g	2g
Apples	52	0g	0g	14g	2g
Raspberries	52	1g	1g	12g	6g
Kale	50	1g	3g	10g	2g
Pineapple	50	0g	1g	13g	1g
Apricots	48	0g	1g	11g	2g
Artichokes	47	0g	3g	11g	5g
Oranges	47	0g	1g	12g	2g
Cranberries	46	0g	0g	12g	5g
Beets	43	0g	2g	10g	3g
Blackberries	43	0g	1g	10g	5g
Celeriac	42	0g	1g	9g	2g
Grapefruit	42	0g	1g	11g	2g
Sugar Snap Peas	42	0g	3g	8g	3g
Carrots	41	0g	1g	10g	3g
Acorn Squash	40	0g	1g	10g	1g
Onion	40	0g	1g	9g	2g
Papaya	39	0g	1g	10g	2g
Peaches	39	0g	1g	10g	1g
Mushrooms	37	0g	2g	7g	3g
Honeydew	36	0g	1g	9g	1g
Rutabagas	36	0g	1g	8g	3g
Broccoli	34	0g	3g	7g	3g
Cantaloupe	34	0g	1g	9g	1g
Serrano Pepper	32	0g	2g	8g	4g
Strawberries	32	0g	1g	8g	2g
Green Beans	31	0g	2g	7g	3g
Okra	31	0g	2g	7g	3g
Spaghetti Squash	31	1g	1g	7g	0g
Sweet Red Peppers	31	0g	1g	6g	2g
Collards	30	0g	2g	6g	4g
Limes	30	0g	1g	11g	3g
Watermelon	30	0g	1g	8g	0g
Lemons	29	0g	1g	9g	3g
Turnips	28	0g	1g	6g	2g
Banana Peppers	27	0g	2g	5g	3g
Sweet Yellow Peppers	27	0g	1g	6g	1g
Mustard Greens	26	0g	3g	5g	3g
Cabbage	25	0g	1g	6g	3g
Cauliflower	25	0g	2g	5g	3g
Eggplant	24	0g	1g	6g	g
Spinach	23	0g	3g	4g	2g
Rhubarb	21	0g	1g	5g	2g

Asparagus	20	0g	2g	4g	2g
Sweet Green Pepper	20	0g	1g	5g	2g
Swiss Chard	19	0g	2g	4g	2g
Tomatoes	18	0g	1g	4g	1g
Celery	16	0g	1g	3g	2g
Radish	16	0g	1g	3g	2g
Summer Squash	16	0g	1g	3g	1g
Cucumbers	15	0g	1g	4g	0g
Lettuce	15	0g	1g	3g	1g

Meat and Poultry

3 oz of cooked food	Calories	Fat	Protein
Chicken (with skin)			
Wing, roasted	240	16g	23g
Thigh, roasted	210	13g	21g
Whole, without neck and giblets, roasted	200	11g	23g
Drumstick, roasted	180	9g	23g
Breast, roasted	170	7g	25g
Turkey (with skin)			
Wing, roasted	190	10g	23g
Thigh, roasted	190	10g	23g
Drumstick, roasted	170	8g	23g
Whole, without neck and giblets, roasted	170	8g	24g
Breast, roasted	160	6g	24g
Beef (with fat trimmed to 1/8 inch)			
Rib, roast, large end, roasted	300	24g	19g
Brisket, point half, braised	300	23g	21g
Chuck, blade roast, braised	290	21g	22g
Brisket, whole, braised	280	21g	22g
Brisket, flat half, braised	250	16g	25g
Chuck, arm pot roast, braised	250	16g	25g
Rib, steak, small end, broiled	240	17g	22g
Loin, top loin steak, broiled	220	14g	22g
Loin, tenderloin steak, broiled	220	14g	22g
Round, bottom round steak, braised	210	10g	28g
Loin, sirloin steak, broiled	200	12g	23g
Round, tip roast, roasted	180	10g	23g
Round, eye round steak, roasted	170	8g	24g
Round, top round steak, broiled	170	8g	26g
Pork			
Spareribs, braised	330	25g	24g
Loin, country style ribs, roasted	280	21g	20g
Shoulder, blade steak, broiled	220	15g	21g
Loin, sirloin roast, roasted	190	11g	22g
Loin, rib chop, broiled	190	11g	21g
Loin, chop, broiled	180	9g	22g
Loin, top loin chop, boneless, broiled	160	8g	22g

Loin, top roast, boneless, roasted	160	7g	22g
Loin tenderloin, roasted	120	3.5g	22g
Lamb (with fat trimmed to 1/8 inch)			
Rib roast, roasted	290	23g	18g
Shoulder, blade chop, broiled	280	20g	24g
Shoulder, arm chop, broiled	280	19g	26g
Loin chop, broiled	250	17g	22g
Leg, sirloin half, roasted	240	17g	21g
Leg, whole, roasted	200	12g	22g
Shank, roasted	180	10g	22g
Leg, shank half, roasted	180	10g	23g

Fish & Seafood

3 oz of cooked food	Calories	Fat	Protein	Carbs
Blue Carb	100	1g	20g	0g
Catfish	130	6g	17g	0g
Clams	110	1.5g	17g	6g
Cod	90	1g	20g	0g
Flounder/Sole	100	1.5g	19g	0g
Haddock	100	1g	21g	0g
Halibut	120	2g	23g	0g
Lobster	80	0.5g	17g	1g
Ocean Perch	110	2g	21g	0g
Orange Roughy	80	1g	16g	0g
Oysters, 12 medium	100	4g	10g	6g
Pollock	90	1g	20g	0g
Rainbow Trout	140	6g	20g	0g
Rockfish	110	2g	21g	0g
Salmon	200	10g	24g	0g
Scallops, 6 large	140	1g	27g	5g
Shrimp	100	1.5g	21g	0g
Swordfish	120	6g	16g	0g
Tilapia	110	2.5g	22g	0g
Tuna	130	1.5g	26g	0g

Conclusion

The instant pot is so versatile and easy to use. Hours of cooking ease and fun, convenience and creativity can color your experience with this amazing appliance. The recipes in this book will provide you and your family with hours of culinary joy. So many recipes are here for you to discover.

Note from the author:

If you've enjoyed this book, I'd greatly appreciate if you could leave an honest review on Amazon.

Reviews are very important to us authors, and it only takes a minute to post.

Thank you

Made in the USA
Lexington, KY
08 December 2016